You're My Parents

By

Clyde Richards

With

Sheryl Richards
and Jake Richards

You're My Parents

Published by Pine Haven Press
614 7th Street
Altavista, Virginia 24517
434-309-7248
php_ink@verizon.net

ISBN   978-0-9789337-7-7
Library of Congress Control Number 2010925501

Printed in the USA

I wish to give credit and thanks to the following people for their part in bringing *You're My Parents* to completion. I could never have done it without their help.

Jake Richards - for typing my rough draft.

Ginger S. - for proof reading my rough draft.

Ruth O. - for editing and preparing the manuscript for printing.

Kevin and Sonya D. - for printing/publishing.

Contents

Endorsements

Much of the story you are about to read will seem unbelievable, but you can believe it. I know I do. After all, I was there and played a small part in this amazing story of international intrigue, lies, deceptions, faith, redemption, and most of all, love.

In some ways, it seems as if the events of this book happened a hundred years ago when actually it has only been a few. Shana, the focus of this book, is now a happily married and well-adjusted wife and mother. Her life, today, is quite normal, but it didn't start off that way.

I first met Shana when Clyde and Sheryl enrolled her in the school in which I was principal. Little did I know, on that uneventful day what the association would mean: court hearings, rumors of our planting snipers on the roof of our Christian school to assassinate Shana's birth father and ultimately being part of a lawsuit in the amount of one hundred million-dollars, which was filed twice, first in District Court and then again in Federal Court. These lawsuits were both dismissed! But these aren't the things I remember the most. What I remember most is the story of overcoming love, faith willing to challenge insurmountable obstacles, and a love that was so big it would not take "impossible" as an answer. It is a story with many characters, but the star is Jesus Christ Himself.

There will be times in which some will be tempted to say, "No way!" But, yes, there was a way. This is a story of that way. This is a story that will entertain, surprise, and amaze you. But most of all it will remind you that faith still moves mountains and love is the most powerful force on the world.

Enjoy the journey.
- Dr. Dan R. / Principal

Shana received Jesus Christ as her Lord and Savior when she was four years of age (a few months before her second abduction). Naturally, when she arrived back in the U.S.A. (two weeks prior to her ninth birthday), she was anxious to resume her relationship with and service for her Lord. She joined the youth department at our church, and by the time she reached her teens, she was very active on the TNT (Teens-N-Touch) ministry team. This team visited other churches, correctional centers, prisons, etc., putting on programs consisting of drama, comedy, martial arts, and other activities that illustrate the advantages of serving Christ.

As her youth pastor, I was impressed by her punctuality, enthusiasm, talent, and willingness to do whatever she could or was asked to do for the team even sharing her thoughts and ideas along this line with me. The team held a number of fund raising activities to pay for their transportation to Mexico where they visited the missionaries and put on programs to help reach Mexicans for Christ, and Shana even led some to Christ herself through this ministry. While on these trips she said she learned to dodge rattlesnakes and cactuses.

Shana seemed to be a natural leader having a confident, exuberant personality that was contagious to those who knew her. Only God could have brought her through her ordeal without psychological scars and made her the type of person she has become, and she gives Him credit for this. *YOU'RE MY PARENTS* is an intriguing true story that glorifies our miracle-working God, for His involvement can be seen throughout.
- James L. / Youth Pastor

I had the privilege of teaching Shana in kindergarten when she was just three years old. She was a beautiful little girl with long black naturally curly hair, and big beautiful dark brown eyes to match. She was very shy and quiet, but I could always tell she was listening to everything and taking it all in. She was a very intelligent and quick learner and was awarded the model student trophy in K3 and K4.

One thing that sticks out in my mind about Shana is how hard it was to get her to say her Bible verse each Friday. She knew the verses, but because she was so shy, she wouldn't speak out loud. I would have to let her whisper them in my ear in order for her to say them. She was always so quiet that I didn't believe she really ever spoke. Clyde and Sheryl said she never stopped talking at home. One time we all went to a local lake together. It was there I got to hear her in action. She was very animated and excited and talked a mile a minute. She was a pleasure to teach and I loved seeing her with her own precious little boy when she visited Clyde in 2007. Only God could have preserved her through her tumultuous childhood and provided her with the perseverance, determination, and faith that have made her the intelligent, well-adjusted wife and mother she is today without any physiological hang-ups or scars. To Him be all the glory!!

- Mrs. J. B. / Teacher

I have known Clyde and Sheryl Richards for over forty years. They have faithfully served the Lord in several areas at the church where I was co-pastor before being called into full-time evangelism.

After raising their own biological children, the Lord brought Shana, a beautiful little girl, into their home. Clyde and Sheryl not only provided a lot of loving care for her, but also provided, for the first time in her young life, a home with stability and a Christian education that she would not have had with her biological father.

Shana professed to receive Jesus Christ as her Lord and Savior at four years of age and expressed her desire to follow her Lord in Believer's baptism by immersion. I had the privilege of baptizing her. Shana has grown into a beautiful young woman, has married, and has a lovely family.

Clyde and his late wife, Sheryl, have been richly blessed by being chosen of God to invest their lives in giving Shana a chance in life she probably would never have had otherwise. To God be the glory!!

- E. C. / Evangelist.

Introduction

You're My Parents is a true story of an adorable little girl named Shana. While Shana is naturally the subject of our story her biological father is essentially the principal character. It was his unusual lifestyle and bizarre activities, which triggered or set in motion most of the events contained herein. It has been said that fact is sometimes stranger than fiction and *You're My Parents* is a prime example of this truth.

While we realize that the inclusion of actual court orders, news article, and photos would add interest to the story, we have been obliged to omit them in an effort to protect the identity of those involved.

The principal characters (names are changed) are as follows:

Shana Simon - subject child
Ron Simon - subject child's biological father
Margaret Simon - Ron Simon's mother
Pearl Simon -   Ron Simon's stepmother
Craig Simon - Ron's brother
Annette Simon - Ron's first wife, mother of first 2 children
Rafiah Simon - Ron's second wife, Shana's mother
Dorothy Simon - Ron's third wife, Milton's mother
Milton Simon - Ron's son by Dorothy
Oshia Simon - Ron's fourth wife
Jinny Simon - Ron's daughter by Oshia
Maria Simon - Ron's fifth wife
Clyde and Sheryl Richards - Shana's court appointed custodians
Landen Richards - Elder son of Clyde and Sheryl
Jake Richards - Younger son of Clyde and Sheryl

Alma - Sheryl's sister
Attorney Franklin - Custodian's first attorney
Attorney Lana Davis - Custodian's second attorney
Rodger Grimes - Social Services Case Worker
Willard Parker - Commonwealth's Attorney
Judge Jacobs - Juvenile and Domestic Relations Court Judge
Judge Goode - Circuit Court Judge

Chapter 1

Ron Simon's Background

Not a lot is known about Ron Simon's background, nor have we investigated this in depth for we are not attempting to analyze if or how his adolescent training may have influenced his adult behavior, but simply to relate a true story as it happened. Ron and his brother Craig relayed to us what information we do have.

It appears that Ron and Craig were born in or near Richmond, Virginia and later, as teenagers, moved to Lynchburg, Virginia, where they attended and finished school. During this time, their parents separated and later divorced because their mother, Margaret Simon, wanted to buy a house in her name. At that time, a Virginia law prevented her from doing this as long as she was married. Both of their parents were professionals. Their mother was a psychiatrist and their father was a lawyer who was a special investigator for the Internal Revenue Service.

Shortly after finishing high school, Ron enrolled in Berkley University at Berkley, California. Years later he told his daughter, Shana, that he had majored in mathematics and, by some news accounts, we believe he may have studied criminology. Perhaps this might explain why he is so adept at filing lawsuits. Apparently the two brothers did not get along very well, so Craig said that he chose not to attend the same high school that Ron was attending until Ron had finished and moved on.

At one point, Craig later testified in court that, "Ron has no mor-

15

als whatsoever."

Perhaps this early character flaw led Ron to get involved with the San Francisco Freedom Sexual League for which he wrote several articles, some of which he sent to Craig.

"They were so filthy my wife made me throw them away," Craig stated.

Apparently, this involvement embarrassed officials at Berkley, (a liberal university by most accounts) to the point that they invited Ron to leave or be dismissed, or so he told Sheryl's sister, Alma. Later, he wound up in New York where he said he worked in the stock market.

Ron may have had one or more mistresses while living in New York. We cannot confirm this, but it would tend to blend with his character. On one occasion, he was driving one of his girlfriends to catch a boat home to Iceland, when his mother's old Volkswagen broke down on the road. As he attempted to summon help, he said a drunk driver hit him breaking both of his legs and his left shoulder, then that driver left the scene. Since it was very cold at the time, he suffered some frostbite on his toes in addition to other injuries by the time help did arrive. After spending some time in a New York hospital, he was transported to his mother's home in Lynchburg, Virginia. It was during this recuperation period in Lynchburg that we first met Ron.

My sister-in-law, Alma, had received a temporary lay-off from her job at a local factory. While Alma was laid-off, she applied for a practical nursing job through a local nursing agency and got the job tending to Ron. After a couple of weeks or so, Alma was called back to her factory job. Since she only needed to work a couple more weeks to retire, Alma asked Sheryl, who was temporarily unemployed, if she would fill in for her so she could return to the nursing job after retirement. Little did we know then how this chance meeting with Ron Simon would affect the rest of our lives, but things began to get more complex and more challenging as our story continues.

The next chapter, "When First We Met," is credited to my wife Sheryl, who can best describe first hand her experiences with and impressions of Ron Simon.

Chapter 2

When First We Met
(By Sheryl Richards)

Mrs. Simon, a well-known psychiatrist who had practiced many years in Lynchburg and was now working in a state hospital some distance away, needed someone to look after her son, Ron. Alma had the responsibility of looking after him while his arm and legs were still in casts. She fixed his meals, helped with his bath, and did all of the necessary menial tasks required in this type of situation. Then, two weeks before she was to retire, Alma was called back to work at the factory. That's when she called me.

At the time, I was not working full-time. I only worked on an "on call" basis in the bookkeeping department of a popular motel chain. When Alma asked me to fill in for her, I readily agreed. Little did I realize then how meeting this man, the intriguing Ron Simon, would change my life.

When I first saw Ron, I felt sorry for him. He was literally helpless. He was a thin, wiry young man in his mid-thirties with dark hair and eyes, but embodied in the enormous casts, Ron seemed almost like a little boy. Ron was a very intelligent man, had traveled a lot, and was very interesting to talk with. He learned that I had secretarial experience, so he asked me to do some typing for him, which I agreed to do, and continued to do even after Alma returned to the health care position after her retirement.

Ron was in a legal battle with the Securities and Exchange Commission at the time and was fighting the system to keep his stockbroker's license, which had been suspended or revoked. I typed many legal briefs over the next year as Ron spent his time busily busily preparing the handwritten rough drafts. During that time, my family and the Simon family became good friends.

Ron and I discussed many topics. He was interested in stocks and bonds, which I did not understand much about. My husband, whom he had met, was in the process of building a small experimental airplane in our basement. Ron thought this to be unusual and pointless. On several occasions we took Ron out just to get him away from the seemingly endless boredom of his at-home confinement.

During his recuperation period, I observed some weird behavioral patterns, which I thought quite strange. For example, he would peel dead skin from his legs where the casts stopped and deposit it on an old newspaper, but when I attempted to discard the skin he would pitch a fit. Apparently, he wanted to save it, but why I do not know! How long he saved it or where it eventually ended up, I have no idea, but I thought it quite weird.

He also seemed to get quite agitated when the telephone rang and he was not able to answer it. The phone was on the main floor, and he was staying in an upstairs bedroom. On one occasion, I answered the phone when his father called. I explained that Ron could not come to the phone right then and asked him to call back later. Ron was so immensely upset that he began to scold me. Obviously, it would be a formidable task and consume quite a bit of time helping him to maneuver down the stairs and get to the telephone in his casts. Ron's scolding, for what I thought was a proper approach, hurt my feelings, and I began to show my displeasure by tossing pillows and jerking sheets as I made up his bed. My actions got his attention and he proceeded to try to calm me down, though he never apologized for his rudeness.

Once, while his friend Celia was visiting from Iceland, we took her to the lake for a picnic along with our boys. Then on the Fourth of July, we took both Ron and Celia, along with our boys, in our old pickup truck for an outing and picnic at a local farm. There was a fireworks display that evening as well as live music. We all had a great time and even Ron, with casts and crutches, seemed to enjoy the festivities.

Eventually, when his casts were removed, Ron decided to return to New York, which was a much more exciting place for him than the small conservative town of Lynchburg. After settling into his apartment in New York, he would still send papers for me to type. These were usually in the form of briefs since his legal battle with the Securities and Exchange Commission was still in progress. These were always of an urgent nature. Rough drafts were sent to me by express mail, and many times I made special trips to the airport to make sure the typed documents were on an airplane for speedy delivery to him.

The work was interesting, I could work from home, and the extra money was nice. The content of the briefs was pretty much dull and boring and most of the time was over my head, but I enjoyed typing and continued to work for him for approximately two or three years. Then Ron decided he was going to travel abroad.

There are many events that took place during a period of time when I did not hear from him. That, I am sure, would be another whole story. However, from time to time, I would receive a postcard from some foreign country just saying "Hi" to our family.

Several years later, Ron was back in the States for a brief period and dropped by the house to see us one evening. His accounts of the experiences he had while traveling overseas were graphic and intriguing as usual.

The tales he told seemed almost unbelievable. After he left that day, I did not hear from him again until one hot July evening in 1982 and that is really where our story begins.

Chapter 3

A Home for Shana

We did not hear anything from Ron for several years since Sheryl's typing assignments were completed in the mid-seventies. Then one night in July 1982, he called and asked Sheryl if she could find him a baby-sitter for a nine-month-old baby girl while he tended to some business. He needed the baby-sitter for a couple of weeks. He sounded pretty desperate as he said, "Whatever they charge, I'll double it."

"Do you have custody of her?" Sheryl asked suspiciously.

I'm sure she meant *legal* custody whether she specifically worded her question that way or not.

His reply was "Yes."

Actually, it would have made little or no difference to him since he would no doubt have said "Yes" anyway. In reality, he did not have full legal custody of his own daughter at that time, or for that matter, any time since. The New York Supreme Court in the county of Bronx had divested him of custody in favor of the mother, however, we were not aware of this at that time.

"Give me a phone number where I can reach you and I'll see what I can do," Sheryl instructed.

Coincidentally, our elder son Landen was temporarily between jobs and he and his wife Lisa were at our house that night.

"Oh, we can do it. Landen can help me," our daughter-in-law insisted. "Besides, we can use the money."

Ron had paid Sheryl adequately for typing, and they thought he was serious about paying double. They had a seven month old son, so they would already be up a lot at night they figured. Besides, it would only be for a couple of weeks.

We could never have imagined at that time what would transpire over the next twelve years (1982-1994), and how it would impact our lives indefinitely. Had we known, we probably would have panicked and exclaimed, "Dear God, surely you don't expect us to go through that!"

Fortunately, God does not show us everything we might encounter at the beginning or some of us would balk at doing His will. He just leads us one day at a time and always goes before us to prepare the way. Romans 8:28 is still true: "And we know that all things work together for good to them that love God, to them who are the called according to His purpose." Many times we wondered how this situation was going to work out for our good when our nerves were frayed and we were on the verge of financial collapse, but God has been with us through it all and we now realize that Shana was one of "His called" and it was working together for her good as well as ours.

After some consultation, our son and daughter-in-law agreed to baby-sit and Sheryl returned Ron's call and told him to "bring her on." Sheryl confided that while waiting for them to arrive she was slightly apprehensive, wondering what the child would look like. I was working the night shift at the time and did not see Shana until the next day. We were all pleasantly surprised. She was a beautiful baby girl with olive skin, a head full of long, dark mahogany ringlets, and great big dark eyes to match. As was the custom of Pakistanis, her arms were adorned with silver colored bracelets.

Being total strangers to her, we did what many would do to get her to respond and laugh at us by making funny faces and sounds, but she was expressionless - like a zombie. Her only response was to try to poke us in the eye or pinch our noses if we got close enough. This behavior continued for a week or so then a miraculous change took place. One night, Lisa, our grandson Jon, and Shana were all gathered at our house and while the women were in the kitchen doing some baking or cleaning for a special occasion, it became my responsibility to keep the children from getting underfoot. To accomplish this, I got on my hands and knees and blocked the exit from the living room where they were confined. Acting like a goat, I would "baa-baa" and gently butt heads with them. After a few such head butts Shana began to laugh and eventually came out of her shell. Since that incident, she has been as normal and affectionate as any child except that she has been reluctant to respond to adults with whom she was not familiar. That caused us a little concern along the way with the lawyers, judges, and social workers that had to deal with this situation, but we have been assured that many other children are that way and it was not abnormal considering what Shana had been through. I can't blame her for not trusting some adults.

My heart aches for children who are victims of broken homes whose parents, for whatever reason, are not mature enough to work out their differences and provide stability for the children they bring into this world. Children have no control over who their parents are or the circumstances that brought them into this world. We did not realize at first that God wanted us to make a permanent home for Shana. After the original two weeks time had passed and our situation continued for several months, and it looked as if it might continue much longer, we felt a responsibility to lay a solid foundation to help her deal with this 'broken home syndrome' which she would ultimately have to face someday if her parents were not reunited. In doing this, we showed her lots of love in order to let her know she was loved and wanted. Loving her was easy and quite rewarding as Shana was very affectionate and returned our love spontaneously.

After Shana had been with our family several weeks longer than the planned two to three weeks, Landen returned to work. Realizing that he needed his rest, they decided they would not be able to continue keeping Shana full time.

Sheryl told Lisa, "If you can keep her during the day, I will keep her at night."

This agreement was temporary until some other arrangement could be worked out. At this time Ron, did not have the means to provide for Shana since he did not even have a job. He was staying at his mother's house and he persuaded his mother to make deposits to his account so he could write checks to 'cash' for Shana's care without letting her know who was keeping Shana.

When Shana was about two years old (maybe before), our daughter-in-law had decided there was too much demand on her time trying to keep another baby so we found another baby-sitter to keep Shana. By the time Shana turned three, we discovered we could enroll her in a Christian kindergarten where she could be learning in a Christian environment. She progressed so well that her teachers selected her for the model student award in K-3 and K-4.

Ron asked us at first not to reveal her last name since it might embarrass his mother. Obviously, she did not approve of his life-style. Most people knew little about the situation and since she preferred to use our last name and sign her papers that way, some may have thought we had adopted her. In fact, she told us one time she wished we would, but it would have required the unanimous consent of both parents, which would have been next to impossible. Plus, it would have cost us more than we could afford. As a result of this misunderstanding, those responsible for the trophies did not have accurate information and our last name was printed on the trophies. Even though we had nothing to do with this error, Ron took exception to it and claimed we were trying to steal his daughter by telling her she was ours.

Chapter 4

First Abduction

During the first few weeks of Shana's stay, Ron revealed that he had abducted Shana from her mother in New York. He had accomplished the abduction by renting a second car, parking it in a conspicuous place where it could be seen and watched, and then parked his other car on another street where it would be unnoticed. During the visitation in a Muslim mosque without the mother's presence, (in violation of the court order), while the Pakistanis/Muslims were having a discussion in another room, Ron slipped out the side door in only his socks (shoes had to be removed in the mosque), climbed over a pile of broken bricks that injured his feet, and then escaped with Shana in the unnoticed car before the others realized what was going on. This was the first abduction and this was when he brought her to us.

Ron arrived at our house driving his mother's old Volkswagen. Also, it was revealed later, that during a custody hearing in a New York Supreme Court, the court ruled in the mother's favor giving her custody of Shana providing she remain in the United States with the baby during her childhood. This was only one or two months before Ron abducted Shana. He said he did it because he was afraid Shana would be taken back to Pakistan. In any case, it was 'parental abduction' which according to Ron, was only a misdemeanor in New York (a felony in Virginia) and for this reason there was very little effort to locate the child. Obviously, if we had known the background facts of this case, we would probably never have gotten involved. We might have panicked and missed a blessing from God.

Shana's mother, Rafiah, being a young woman in a strange country, not speaking the language nor understanding the customs, and having been abused on her honeymoon according to her testimony in court, wanted to return to her country and to her people. She did not abandon Shana as Ron later tried to convince the courts He told us he instigated deportation proceedings against her and paid for her ticket back to Pakistan. Ron preyed on her beliefs. According to the customs of her religion, the fathers 'own' the children and the mothers have little or no rights. Even if she could raise the necessary support to finally have Shana returned to her, which she probably couldn't have, and the funds to return to Pakistan where there was no welfare to help, she would probably have been frowned upon as an unfaithful wife and may have had difficulty finding a decent husband. She has since gotten a divorce or annulment from Ron, married a Pakistani lawyer, lives in Pakistan and has three more children at last report. We try to maintain contact through mutual acquaintances.

A few other interesting tidbits of information: Ron bragged to his brother Craig that he had bought Rafiah, for a dowry of fifteen hundred dollars. She was a beautiful orphaned Pakistani Muslim girl. After Ron had fled New York with Shana, he first went to Craig's house in North Carolina. When they arrived, Craig's wife said that Shana's diaper was "wet and dirty." Apparently, Margaret Simon, Ron's mother, had been in New York during the custody proceedings and for fear that Ron might get in serious trouble for abducting the child in violation of the order of the New York Supreme Court, called authorities in New York and informed them of Shana's whereabouts. When the representative from New York arrived at Craig's house to retrieve Shana, Ron then fled to the northern part of the Shenandoah Valley of Virginia to some acquaintances there and that is where he was when he called Sheryl.

After Shana had been with us for about a month or two, Ron received a threatening note presumably from the Black Muslim Militant Underground Organization (B.M.M.U.O.) giving him an ultimatum and warning him that if he did not strictly abide by its terms they would send out their hit squad and have him brutally murdered. "You will feel the sting of our Stilettos," it read. I do not remember all of the terms or instructions in the note, but one order was that he was to return Shana to the New York court's jurisdiction and another was to the effect that he was to cease all contact with and abuse of the Muslim 'sisters.'

Ron was given a time limit to comply and with the stipulation that there were to be no deviations. He later claimed that he discovered it was written by one of Rafiah's relatives who was attending a university in Canada, but at the time Ron received the orders he was taking it very seriously. He contacted the local police and the F. B. I., but they told him they could take no action unless a crime had been committed. Apparently, they didn't feel that a threat on his life was a crime, especially under the circumstances. Obviously, they knew him better than we did at the time.

It was at this point that his mother's old Volkswagen kicked the bucket and Ron was left without transportation of his own. Being paranoid as he was, and customarily blaming others for his problems, he theorized that someone had sabotaged the beetle by putting sand or sugar in the crankcase and requested that the mechanic at the VW dealership have the oil analyzed, but the mechanic refused and left that option open to Ron if he chose to pursue it. Actually, the car had over 100,000 miles on it according to Ron and probably had only minimum maintenance, if any.

I was working day shift at the time and made several trips to town (about six miles) after work to pick him up and bring him to our house so he could visit with Shana. She expressed very little emotion or affection towards Ron during these visits. She just played with his glasses or tugged at his nose, but this was probably because she didn't see much of him during this part of her life. He was basically a stranger to her. As the time limit of the Muslim militant ultimatum drew near, Ron began to get anxious because he had no transportation. Eventually, he found a used car at the same VW dealership that had checked his mother's bug when it broke down. He seemed to be somewhat relieved now that he had some means of conveyance, but about a week before the actual deadline, the transmission went bad in that car and he began to sweat it saying that he didn't have the money to get it fixed. However, he got money from somewhere, probably his mother or some family friends, because he got the car fixed and left town the day before the deadline.

We got a call from him a couple of days later claiming he was at the Texas stadium watching a Dallas Cowboy's football game. After that, we didn't hear from him for nearly a year, and we had no idea where he was. We learned later that he wound up in El Salvador. It seems that Ron had a knack for winding up in the hot spots of the world amid conflict: first, in El Salvador and then later in Afghanistan. This fostered our suspicion that he was employed by the CIA since he was able to get in and out of these situations, even though he was jailed several times for short periods and had over twenty complaints filed against him with the U. S. State Department by host countries.

While he was in El Salvador or a neighboring country, he contacted the New York Supreme Court claiming that Rafiah had abandoned Shana and returned to Pakistan. Therefore, he was seeking a reversal of the custody order thereby giving him legal custody of Shana. Actually, he had Rafiah sent back to Pakistan he told us, "to keep her out of his hair" hoping to patch things up later. The New York Court, aware that Ron had abducted Shana in violation of its order, was reluctant to do so, but did contact the Department of Social Services or Court Services with a request to investigate Shana's welfare and living conditions. The DSS knew she was in the area and could have located her if they had been determined to do so. If they had submitted a letter to the Lynchburg area newspaper requesting information about her, we would certainly have responded rather than risk charges of withholding information or obstructing justice.

Like Ron, we were concerned about the possibility of Shana being taken to Pakistan, but for a very different reason. Of course, we were at first hopeful that her parents would be reunited so she would not have her confidence shattered by those whom she should have been able to count on for stability, but this was not to be. God had other plans. Being children of God by the 'new birth' as commanded by Jesus in the Gospel of John (John 1:12, 13, 3:7) we considered things from His perspective. We remembered that God "would have all men to be saved, and come unto the knowledge of the truth" (I Timothy 2:4). This includes women and children old enough to respond as well as Ron who had previously been invited to do so. And we knew it was God's will for Shana to have this opportunity.

With this in mind, I prayed, "Lord, it would be a shame for this adorable, lovable, innocent child to be taken back into this heathen, idolatrous culture, grow up there, and spend eternity in Hell, never having had an opportunity to hear the Gospel of Jesus Christ and be saved." (Romans 1:16)

I am not one of these weird Christians who believe that God speaks to us audibly, giving new revelations, but I do believe that His Spirit of Truth bears witness with our spirit (John 16:13, Romans 8:16) and persuades or influences our minds (Galatians 5:8, Ephesians 4:23) through His Word and gives His children direction and wisdom in making difficult decisions.

When I prayed, in the aforementioned manner to the Lord, His response was clear. "My sentiments exactly. Why do you think I had her placed in your care?"

Needless to say, this was a very humbling revelation. To be made aware of God's direct leadership and purpose for one's life will not make the believer proud in his heart, but will humble him and draw him closer to God as he seeks to follow His leadership as never before.

Even with this awareness, we did not approach the situation any differently, although Sheryl was inclined to ask on several occasions, "Why us Lord?"

To which I would respond in an effort to encourage her, "Why not us? Who is better prepared to make a home for Shana?"

You may be wondering by now, "Where does Ron get the money to travel all over the world if he doesn't hold a regular job?" This question has been asked hundreds of times since our involvement. Some have theorized that he was a spook employed by the Central Intelligence Agency. Others think this highly unlikely. I have concluded that he is an international 'con artist' even though that still doesn't fully explain how he is able to con so many people out of so much. He frequently makes acquaintances of people of shady character who seem to be well off financially. He wins their confidence to the degree that he is able to prey on their sympathy to meet his needs.

There are two possibilities that might help unravel at least part of this mystery. One is that Ron's father was a special investigator for the Internal Revenue Service and it is my theory that Ron may have picked his father's brain for enough information to help him avoid paying income taxes. He testified under oath in two courts, one in South Carolina and one in Virginia, that he had not paid income taxes in the United States for over twenty years.

The other, and closely connected possibility, is that Ron, being heavily dependent upon his mother, may have laundered money by running it through her bank account by depositing cash or checks and then having her write him checks when he needed money making it difficult, if not impossible, for the IRS to trace. He is known to have borrowed large sums of money from his mother and if he made any profit on his investment, he deposited it back into her bank account. My guess is that he borrowed a lot more than he returned because his mother's Alzheimer's condition made her an easy target. The IRS has been notified about his evasion of taxes, but thus far nothing has been done that I am aware of. I guess they only go after those from whom they think they can recover money.

Chapter 5

Bonding With Shana

Referring back to the New York Court's request for a welfare investigation in Lynchburg, it appears that the Social Services worker assigned to the case knew some members of the family, especially Ron's mother, because Dr. Simon contacted Ron by phone about the request for an investigation. Ron then called the Social Services worker and talked with her before calling Sheryl and asking us to arrange an appointment for the investigation. He asked the Social Services worker if she was willing to be blindfolded so she wouldn't know how to get to our house. He didn't want to take any chances that any information would leak as to Shana's whereabouts, either to the New York courts or to the Pakistani Muslims in New York. Even his mother was deprived of this information, although she was financially providing for Shana's care.

When I arranged to pick up the social worker and bring her to our house I determined, "There is no way I'm going to blindfold this woman. If she has her own blindfold and voluntarily puts it on, I'll take the winding back way home and turn her around, otherwise, I'm not going to do it."

When I met her and had a few words with her, I determined she could be trusted and was not planning to double-cross us, so I confided in her, "You will find that Shana is not living in Lynchburg."

"Oh, I knew that," she replied, then continued, "I read the police report that was filed when Ron received the threat and it stated that she was in the 'vicinity of Lynchburg.'"

She assured me that she would not include our names or address in the report to the New York court, but just the pertinent information about Shana's living conditions. Since she did not apply a blindfold or even appear to have one, I proceeded straight to our house. If she got any information about us, she got it through our license number because she did not ask for nor did we volunteer any.

The case worker very professionally examined our house, including Shana's room, and asked a few basic questions. One question, which particularly impressed me, was "Is she allowed to call you mommy and daddy?"

Sheryl replied, "Yes."

"That's the way it ought to be." The social worker responded.

Actually, it came naturally and seemed appropriate since we were the only mommy and daddy Shana could count on at the time. Almost anyone can become a parent by producing a child, but only those who provide for that child's physical and psychological needs such as feeding, changing, bathing, loving, reading to, and praying with and for them deserve the title mommy and daddy.

Ron was still in Central America during all of this and after spending approximately a year there where several complaints were registered with the U.S. State Department concerning his activities, Ron finally returned to his mother's home in Lynchburg, Virginia. Upon his return, he proceeded to visit Shana a few times before leaving town again. His next mission was to return to Pakistan in an effort to persuade Rafiah to come back to the States with him.

When Sheryl heard about this, she asked Ron, "What are we supposed to do with Shana if some of your enemies do you in while you're gone?"

"I want you to keep her and raise her if anything happens to me," he said, and then wrote a note to confirm his wishes.

Of course, nothing serious happened to him, but this at least revealed his preference of custodians. In Pakistan, having failed in his quest to re-win Rafiah, he attempted to work out a divorce agreement with some of her male relatives, with whom the marriage agreement was first arranged. Before the divorce agreement could be implemented, Ron told us a serious argument ensued, and suspecting that his life was in danger, he fled Pakistan. Later, we received a card from him mailed from somewhere in China and then we heard nothing more for at least a year. Eventually, his mother or his brother told us that he was in Japan where he had gotten a bit part in a movie (he strode across the tarmac in a pilot's uniform). From the time he left for Pakistan to reclaim Rafiah, until he eventually returned to the United States, it was a little over two years. During that time, he had no contact whatsoever with Shana either by phone, letter, card, or gifts on her birthday or at Christmas.

During this period of time, the reimbursement checks he had been sending us ceased. This did not concern us too much since Shana was such a source of joy that we would have provided a home for her for nothing if we could get Ron to agree to let us continue raising her in the stable environment to which she was accustomed. However, as long as we were doing him a service that could be discontinued, reimbursement was in order.

When discussing with Craig the possibility of reasoning with Ron about this situation, Craig replied, "My brother has no reason."

Actually, this seemed the best situation for Shana, him, and us since Ron had no wife to be a motherly figure to love and guide Shana, no home or house in which to live (except his mother's), and no regular job by which to support any of them. His mother had been providing the money for Shana's necessities. Plus, Shana was getting attached to us and we to her.

Ron later claimed in court that he had hired Sheryl as a babysitter and fired her when he discovered we were trying to steal his daughter. I reminded him that the pay, divided by 168 hours (24 hours a day, seven days a week), was less than $0.65 per hour, hardly baby-sitting wages, but with thrifty shopping plus gifts of clothing, toys, etc., we made it work.

The bonding with Shana began with our Billy Goat play and over the years we grew to love her as if she were our own. When she was just a baby, people would approach us for a closer look while we were shopping and exclaim, "What a beautiful baby! Is she your granddaughter?" Now I don't know if Sheryl and I looked old enough to be grandparents, but they could tell she was not our offspring since we were both fair-skinned and light haired with blue/gray eyes while Shana had dark brown ringlets, big dark brown eyes, and an olive complexion.

Our standard answer was, "No, she's more like a foster child." But that was about it because we certainly didn't have time to explain to everyone who might inquire, nor did we fully understand what we had gotten involved in at that time.

Additional evidence of this bonding process was observed on several occasions while riding in the 'car car.' Sheryl and I would be engrossed in conversation or discussion in the front seat thinking that Shana was asleep or preoccupied in the back when suddenly from the back seat came, "Daddy? DADDY? DADDY?!?"

Children are very impatient. They want to be heard NOW. Slightly perturbed by the interruption, I would inquire," What is it now, Shana?"

To which she replied, "I love you."

I don't know of anyone who could be bitter about that. It would melt the hardest of hearts and mine wasn't even hard.

We enjoyed taking her places and doing things with her because she seemed to appreciate it so much. When she was barely a year old, we took her with us to visit my sister in Atlanta, Georgia. Shana was a very good traveler except when she got bored or tired from being strapped in the car seat by herself; in which case, one of us would have to sit in the back seat with her or sneak her into the front seat with us for a little while. Once, when she was two years old, we took her to Virginia Beach where we jumped in the waves together. I got sunburned because she did not want me to put her down.

The next year we took her with us when we took our son Landen's car with a few belongings and escorted his wife and young son to Biloxi, Mississippi, where he was stationed with the United States Air Force. From there we went to New Orleans, Louisiana, where we visited the World's Fair and then visited relatives in DeFuniak Springs, Florida; Albany, Georgia; and Atlanta, Georgia on the way back. We took her everywhere we went, and she seemed to enjoy it so much. We only left her once that I can remember and that was when we left her with a baby-sitter for two or three days while we went on a second honeymoon.

After Dr. Simon was diagnosed as having Alzheimer's, Ron began to feel guilty about not letting his mother know who was keeping Shana, so he called us and told us to share this information with her. When we informed Dr. Simon who we were and that we were taking care of Shana, she was very pleased. Since she knew us from the time of Ron's accident. When we shared with Dr. Simon how much Shana enjoyed the beach, she commented that she and some of her siblings owned an apartment at Myrtle Beach, South Carolina, and that maybe we could take Shana there some day, but there was no firm commitment at the time.

Traveling as much as we did with Shana finally brought to my attention the fact that an injury to her or an emergency medical decision on her behalf could make us vulnerable to a lawsuit from Ron. Since we did not have even temporary legal custody of her, we didn't have a leg to stand on, nor could we carry her on my company insurance policy. In the beginning, Ron had arranged for a local pediatrician to tend to her when needed and have the bill sent to his mother. I don't know if Dr. Simon was a party to this deal or not, but the bills were paid by someone. However, this would not benefit Shana if she were away from home.

Realizing Ron would eventually return and want to take Shana to live with him, we decided it was time to explain the situation to her since she was four years old by this time. I've been told by several people that child psychologists recommend any custodial change in a child's life take place by the time they are two or three years of age if possible. This is because at this age they are less likely to develop psychological scars from such traumas than if this occurs at an older age. We sat down with her and explained to her that we were not her natural parents, but her father had selected us to keep her for him in his absence. Even though the original two to three weeks had multiplied many times over, Ron still seemed to be satisfied with the arrangement.

I don't remember if we told Shana about Ron's abducting her from her mother at this time, but somehow I felt she knew something was amiss. Shana began asking questions about her parents and where they were, especially since she hadn't see her natural mother for nearly four years and had only seen her father a few times during the same period.

We showed Shana pictures her parents.

"Where are they now?" She inquired.

"As far as we know your mother, Rafiah, has returned to Pakistan and is still there, or at least that's what your father told us. He told us he was leaving for Pakistan to try to get her back and we haven't heard from him since, so we don't know exactly where he is right now."

"They don't love me very much do they?" Shana asked.

I'm sure Sheryl had some legitimate doubts about the validity of Ron's love for his daughter, but trying not to speak about him in a derogatory manner, she responded; "Oh, I don't want you to feel like they don't love you. I'm sure they both love you very much, but neither of them wants the other one to have you."

A thoughtful expression came over Shana's face and after a brief pause she spoke in a very serious tone," W-e-l-l, they've lost me, YOU'RE MY PARENTS."

Even though we thought we understood how she felt, this startling declaration electrified us. Certainly we were the only mommy and daddy she had ever really known or could remember since she was nine months old, but when she revealed that she had psychologically adopted us as her parents, it strengthened our inner resolve to defend her decision any way that we could, legally.

Ron knew, long before he ever left Shana with us, that we were Christians and that we did not sit at home on the Lord's day, but would attend church and take Shana with us. There she would be taught the truth from the Word of God as we had been. If he had informed us in the beginning that he wanted her raised Muslim, that would have been a no-no for us from the start because we would never teach such heathen, idolatrous religiosity to any child in our care. Considering the fact that Ron had voluntarily left Shana in our care, knowing our religious convictions, and seemingly content with the situation, coupled with our previously mentioned revelations, it was quite clear to us that God was working out His plan for Shana's life. Craig said Ron told him that he was "kind of glad Shana was being raised in Christianity."

Just a few weeks, perhaps a month or two, before Shana's startling declaration that we were her parents, she had received Jesus Christ, God's Son, as her Lord and Savior. She was under no pressure to do so. She was only four years of age, but did so voluntarily.

Her decision to receive Christ, of course made us very happy and more determined than ever to defend her right to follow Jesus, hopefully in an encouraging environment.

Shortly thereafter she wanted to follow her Lord in believer's baptism (submersion in water after salvation, Acts 2:41). Naturally we rejoiced with her, but because of her age, we desired as best as could be determined, that she understand what she was doing. We asked our associate pastor, with whom she seemed to feel at ease, to question her before the baptism.

We, as a church, do not target children and terrorize them as some might believe, but we do have compassionate teachers who teach them the Word of God on a child's level much like Jesus did. He was compassionate and patient with children and saved His fiery rebukes for the scribes, hypocrites, and Pharisees (religious leaders who were perverting the Scriptures and, of course, had rejected Him, thus leading people astray like most of today's religions). We do, however, have youth leaders who have a burden for young people, because not only do statistics show that the majority of Christians are saved at a tender, young age, but also that a simple, childlike, unfeigned faith is essential to biblical salvation. (Mark 10:14; Luke 16:18; Matthew 18:3; 11:25).

We are warned that the cares of this life, the deceitfulness of sin, the lust for riches and other things can harden a person's heart when he gets older and he becomes unresponsive to God's Word. (Mark 4:19; Hebrews 3:13). Of course, there are many things that young children do not understand when they first trust Jesus Christ to be their Lord and Savior, for they are but babes in Christ (I Corinthians 3:1) and have not yet been faced with adult temptations. But the foundation had been laid (I Corinthians 3:11) and it would be to Shana an anchor throughout her life (Proverbs 22:6).

After our associate pastor talked with Shana and was convinced she understood, he proceeded to baptize her as she had requested. Ron later complained that the pastor performed the 'ritual' of baptism on her making her a Christian. That shows how much he knows/ doesn't know about Christianity. No ritual can make one a Christian; "You must be born again." (John 1:12,13; 3:5-7).

Eventually, we received word that Ron was making his way back to the United States by way of the Philippines. When he returned, a Filipino woman named Maria, whom he introduced as his new wife, accompanied him.

During some later conversations, Sheryl asked him, "Are you legally married?"

He already had two or more mistresses, so marriage to him was not taken too seriously.

"Didn't I tell you she was my wife?" Ron responded, and produced what appeared to be a marriage license.

"Yes, but that doesn't mean I believe you," Sheryl replied.

Finally he admitted the marriage license was a fake. Maria had typed it and he had forged some fictitious names on it. (He proved to be quite adept at forging names, especially his mother's, as we later learned.) Apparently, they used each other - she used him to get into the United States as his wife, and he used her for whatever he could get in return. After a few weeks, Maria flew the coop never to be heard from again to the best of our knowledge.

Since, as was previously mentioned, we had no legal custody of Shana and no legitimate insurance coverage on her in case of an accident on the road, we contacted an attorney about our legal responsibilities. He advised us to try to get Ron to meet with us to see if we could work out some form of temporary custody so that we could put her on our company policy. This would be our first opportunity to solve this dilemma since Ron had been on the move most of the time, and we felt as if it would be better for him, Shana, and us if a solution could be reached that would allow her to remain with us, but at the same time relieve us of unnecessary liabilities.

In the beginning, we had mentioned that we would be willing to adopt Shana, if he would agree in order to provide her with a stable home life, which he apparently was unable or unwilling to provide for her.

"I fully intend to raise my own daughter." He stated, but by this time, he had missed the most formative four years of her life having practically abandoned her, not to mention the fact that she had gotten attached to us and we to her during this period.

We did get Ron to meet us at the attorney's office, but when the attorney mentioned something about temporary custody, Ron repeatedly asked, "How long would that last?"

"Until such time as it is changed." Was the answer. I don't think we fully realized at this time that because the New York court had divested him of the custody of his own daughter and declined to reverse that order, he would not have been any help in providing a solution - in fact, he proceeded to make matters worse. The real shocker came when Ron revealed that he and his mother had concluded (prior to the meeting) that we were simply trying to steal his daughter.

During Ron's absence, he had his mother file for custody of Shana because the New York court had refused his petition for a reversal of the original order. However, she was informed that Lynchburg did not have jurisdiction since it was not the child's place of residence. Shortly after his return, Ron filed a petition for custody in Amherst County where we lived.

Chapter 6

Preliminary Hearings

The attorney we selected to advise us, Mr. Franklin, was recommended by some of my wife's coworkers because of his previous experience with foreign adoptions. We had been the only mommy and daddy she had known for nearly four years. Shana also had declared, "I don't wanna live wiss nobody but y'all!" All this along with the fact that she was accustomed to living in a loving, stable environment, we were naturally concerned about any trauma in her life that might be caused by uprooting her and exposing her to less favorable conditions. We didn't know what kind of life Ron could or would provide for her. We figured it wouldn't be good. Ron had already proven that he was unable or unwilling to provide a decent life for Shana, and she desperately needed that. Neither did he have a regular job, a steady source of income, nor a place to call home except his mother's house where he stayed while in town. He had two other children by his first wife, from whom he was not yet divorced, when he married Rafiah. He was faced with a judgment in excess of $17,000 for back child support. His mother had provided for Shana's needs in the beginning, but her provision had stopped over two years before.

Ron told us when Shana was just a baby that he had received two marriage proposals for her to marry one of his Muslim friend's sons, but Ron did not say that he had made any commitments along this line. With all of these negative uncertainties, we were deeply concerned for Shana's future. Would he sell her to be married to the son of one of his Muslim friends as Rafiah's family had done to her? Would he force Shana into prostitution? We just didn't know.

We knew by now that we didn't trust him. Therefore, we sought the advice of an attorney in case a peaceful solution couldn't be reached and we had to sue for custody of Shana. The attorney told us that our chances of winning custody over a biological parent was practically impossible in Virginia because the laws generally favored placing the child in the custody of a natural parent. If Ron was proven to be unfit as a parent and her mother Rafiah did not file for custody then we might have a chance. He did tell us, however, that there had been a couple of cases in Virginia in recent years that had been won on these grounds.

Meanwhile, our routine during Shana's pre-k and kindergarten years was for Sheryl to drop her off at day care where Sheryl would meet another lady and car-pool to work. Monday through Thursday, I would pick Shana up from school and leave her with Sheryl's sister Alma before I went to work. If for some reason I could not pick up Shana, Sheryl would pick her up on the way home. On Fridays I would pick Shana up at noon and after dropping by the bank, where they would give her suckers, I would take her out for lunch before going to work. She seemed to be happy with this routine and we looked forward to spending time together on the weekends.

However, when Ron wanted to take her for all day visits Shana seemed to be a little uncomfortable since she had not seen him for two years and very little before that. As a result, we recommended that Ron take her for short, fun trips to ease the re-acquaintance process, but he didn't appear to be interested. Regardless of what we had planned he expected us to defer to his whims no matter how inconvenient or how short the notice, even if we had something planned or if Shana were taking a nap. Ron apparently thought he was sovereign. We didn't. We did try to accommodate him as much as possible for Shana's sake and to avoid conflict.

Ron would retrieve his mother from his brother's house in North Carolina to entertain Shana on these visits and to support him financially. His mother had been diagnosed with Alzheimer's and as a result had been forced to retire from her job as a psychiatrist at a psychiatric facility in western Virginia. Ron knew of her diagnosis and told me she had Alzheimer's, but later he would deny it when he thought it was to his advantage to convince others that his mom was of sound mind. What a golden opportunity for him to take control of, manipulate, think, and act for her while trying to convince others that she was acting on her own. He continued in this manner for several years, but those who knew him were not fooled and eventually Craig and an uncle broke up his scheme after Ron had wasted quite a bit of his mother's money.

As the time of the scheduled hearing on Ron's petition for custody approached, our attorney did not want to appear in court that day because "This guy's crazy," he said. "Who knows what he might do if he sees me there representing you? He's already told his brother he would abduct Shana again if you all oppose him over this custody issue."

Mr. Franklin did, however, arrange with the judge to have us subpoenaed so we would have to be in court, but without our lawyer. Although he had not filed a petition for custody on our behalf and we were therefore not a party in the case at this time, we were concerned about Shana's future with her father and the potential emotional and psychological trauma it might put her through.

Ron appeared a little surprised that we were in court, but when Judge Jacobs asked us to explain our involvement, we told him that we were there to plead with the court to do what was best for the child. We knew that if we attempted to tell the judge just what kind of person he was dealing with, he would think we were paranoid and it might go against us. On the other hand, if we could persuade him to investigate Ron's background and lifestyle, he would be reluctant to take Shana from a stable, loving environment where she felt secure and place her in a turbulent situation.

Ron was represented by an attorney who extolled Ron's virtues and bragged about the notoriety Ron had received in New York and Pakistan. He showed us articles from the Pakistani section of the New York Times and from a magazine published in Islamabad, Pakistan, both of which were derogatory toward Ron, but he seemed to thrive on any publicity, regardless of how it portrayed him.

After Judge Jacobs heard about Ron's notoriety, he informed Ron and his attorney that he wanted copies of all information pertaining to this case on his desk first thing the following Monday morning so he could review it. Just to make sure the child would remain within the jurisdiction of the Amherst court, he issued a temporary emergency order citing the Uniform Child Custody Jurisdiction Act and the Federal Parental Kidnapping Act, which in effect, gave us physical custody of Shana and joint legal custody with her father until further notice.

Ron was so paranoid that he requested that our names be omitted from the court order lest his enemies get hold of it and discover Shana's whereabouts. For this reason, the temporary order granted "joint legal custody to the father and present custodians," and ordered that the child "not be removed from the Commonwealth of Virginia, nor her whereabouts kept secret from the Amherst court." This emergency ruling would insure that the situation would remain status quo while efforts were being made to contact Shana's mother and inform her of the proceedings so she could make her wishes known to the court. The Amherst Juvenile and Domestic Relations court would also have to contact the New York Supreme Court which had divested Ron of custody of his daughter one month before he abducted her the first time and request their position on this matter. Whether they would defer jurisdiction to the Virginia courts or whether they would challenge the Virginia court's involvement was unsure.

Another date was then set for a continuation with an interim period allowing time for the necessary contacts to be made. These proceedings began in the spring of 1986 and continued into the summer months. Then the pace began to quicken.

About this time, Ron surprised Sheryl by asking her how she would like to raise a couple more kids (probably his first two) to which she replied: "Do I look like I'm crazy?"

Shortly after the temporary order was handed down, Ron decided he wanted to take Shana on a trip so he called his mother and told her that he was going to bring Shana to visit her. His mother was at that time living with Craig in South Carolina.

When his mother called and awoke me from a deep sleep one morning, she asked, "Did I dream it or did Ron say he was bringing Shana to see me?"

"Sheryl said something about him wanting to bring her to see you, but the court order states that Shana is not to be taken out of the state of Virginia without further order of that court so unless that order is modified he cannot do so legally," I replied.

"I wish he would stop dragging her around like a piece of baggage," lamented Dr. Simon.

Somehow Ron persuaded his lawyer to press Judge Jacobs to sign a modified order late one evening. Failing to reach Sheryl by telephone for a couple of hours, Ron hand delivered the order that night.

According to a telephone conversation, he taped that evening he told his lawyer he was afraid we had skipped out with Shana. I can't imagine why he thought we would try to pull a stunt like that unless it was the fact that he had previously done so and might be contemplating doing it again. We certainly had neither reason nor means to leave town.

The modified court order gave Ron permission to take Shana to visit her grandmother in North Carolina. Ron knew that his mother was living in South Carolina and that was where he would have to go to visit her. At first I thought it must have been a technical error, but later discovered that he had no intention of going to North or South Carolina. Instead, he was headed in the opposite direction. I checked the signature carefully to verify that it matched Judge Jacob's on other court orders to determine if it was legitimate. Even though I concluded that it was, I was stunned by the fact that the judge had not attempted to contact our attorney or us or at least have the order delivered by a deputy rather than sending it by Ron.

It has been one of Ron's characteristics throughout this ordeal to try to push things through at the last minute not allowing opposing parties time to respond, or he would file papers the day before weekends and holidays, giving him time to flee.

When Sheryl informed Shana that her father had received the court's permission to take her to visit her grandmother and we would have to cooperate, Shana cried herself to sleep. I think even she suspected something was wrong and she definitely did not want to go because she didn't feel comfortable with her father. Ron told Sheryl when he delivered the modified order that he expected Shana to be dressed and ready to go by 6:30 the next morning.

When I got home a little after 4:30 a.m., Sheryl was awake and said she hadn't slept much and was upset. I decided to stay up and comfort her as much as I could.

When Sheryl roused Shana and got her dressed the poor little thing was shaking, sobbing, and clutching my finger for dear life as if to say, "Why don't you do something?"

Even though I didn't know what Ron was planning then, it was one of the hardest battles I have ever had with the flesh. I've always tried to be a law-abiding citizen and I knew that if I intervened I could be charged with assault, and lose my standing in court.

Finally, with a broken heart and almost in tears as she clutched my finger, I blurted out "Shana, he knows how you feel, but he just doesn't care."

Eventually Sheryl came to the rescue when she picked Shana up in her arms, carried her to Ron's car, buckled her in, and closed the door with Shana still crying. Then she turned to Ron as he approached the driver's door and told him through her tears, "I hope this haunts you the for rest of your life."

Later in court Ron claimed that we had made derogatory remarks about him in Shana's presence and the judge reprimanded us without even inquiring about what was said, possibly to convince Ron that he was trying to be impartial.

Almost immediately after Ron and Shana left, Sheryl called Craig and his wife in South Carolina and told them, "They're on their way, but Shana is very upset and crying. Please call us when they arrive and let us know how she is doing."

Sheryl had asked Ron before he left whether he would be driving or flying and what time he expected to have her back. He said, "Both." Obviously one couldn't drive to South Carolina and back in one day and have time to visit, too. He said he would have her back by 7:00 - 7:30 that night.

When we had not heard from Craig or his wife by early that afternoon, we called to see how Shana was, only to be told that they had not arrived. Craig checked with the commuter airlines serving their little airport and discovered that there were no schedules that would allow them to fly down, rent a car for a visit, and fly back by the given time. That information caused us much anxiety during the afternoon, but our attorney suggested we try to remain calm and if they had not arrived back by the scheduled time, then call him back.

As the scheduled time passed, we called our attorney who then contacted Ron's attorney, and I think, Judge Jacobs who had modified the order. We emphasized that the child's grandmother did not live in North Carolina where Ron was supposed to have gone, but in South Carolina, yet no one had a clue as to what had happened, whether they had an accident or whether it was one or Ron's elusive schemes.

Around 9:00 p.m., Ron's attorney received a phone call from him claiming he was delayed by a rain/thunder storm north of Charlottesville, Virginia. Charlottesville?!! That's the opposite direction from Aiken, South Carolina. We knew for sure then that we had been bamboozled. We were convinced that Ron could not be trusted, but the judge had to learn for himself. As it turned out, Ron had an appointment with a child psychologist in New York where, according to Craig, Ron was to have a supervised visit with his first two children. He had already lost the right to unsupervised visits and eventually lost all visitation rights. His first wife had remarried after their divorce and sued him for child support, which to the best of our knowledge is still unpaid. Ron has at least seven children by four different women that we are aware of and isn't supporting any of them. According to Craig, the purpose of this visit was to show the psychologist how calm and well-behaved Shana was (under his care) compared to the other two who were apparently quite hyper and suggest they be placed in his custody. Most likely these were the other two he wanted Sheryl to raise.

Ron eventually brought Shana back to us. He was supposed to have her back by 7:00 in the evening, but it ended up being more like 9:00.

Chapter 7

Second Abduction

When the date of the next scheduled court appearance came, the court had received no word from Shana's mother and could not go forward with the custody issue without making another attempt to contact her. Ron explained that she was from a remote village up in the Himalayan mountains of northern Pakistan where mail delivery was very slow. That, coupled with the fact that someone else would have to write or translate for her, it could take some time to hear from her. In the meantime, however, Ron, pressed by the delusion that his daughter was gifted or his desire to rescue her from our care, requested permission from the court to remove her from Temple Christian School and enroll her in an advanced school for gifted children. While another attempt was being made to contact Rafiah, Judge Jacobs decided to tackle the school issue.

It just so happened that on this day Sheryl had taken Shana to her work office to be picked up for visitation, a plan that had been agreed upon by all parties except Ron, who, while desiring visitation, didn't think his sovereign rights should be restricted in any way. He failed to realize this was America and not a Muslim ruled country. Besides, there was a valid question regarding his legitimacy as a Muslim. Sheryl described the scene at her office that day when Ron arrived to pick her up. Shana stayed right behind Sheryl until she told her that her workday had begun and that Shana could not follow her around all day. Shana then sat down in a corner and would not budge until Ron picked her up and told her, "This is the way it has to be," and carried her from the office kicking and cry-ing - a scene that haunted all those who witnessed it for years to come. He later claimed that we had put her up to it. In reality, it was a natural reaction for a frightened child. Perhaps Shana had sensed that something was going to happen.

Later that same day in court, our attorney, Mr. Franklin, was there to represent us as we had expressed to him our disapproval of the transfer. The two attorneys were invited into the judge's cham-bers to discuss the issue while we stayed in the waiting room. Ron was visibly upset and impatient because he was not allowed to take part in the discussion. He paced back and forth with his heel taps clicking on the cement floor. Even though we tried to remain calm and collected, I was tempted several times to tell him to, "Sit down and be quiet - you're making me nervous."

We would not have been human if we hadn't been concerned about each decision in this case, but we were comforted by these words: "The king's heart is in the hand of the Lord, as the rivers of water; he turneth it whithersoever he will" (Proverbs 21:1). If the king's heart was in the Lord's hands, certainly the judge's was and the Lord would bring about the decision He wanted.

Both Ron and his mother appeared in court together, which meant that someone else was keeping Shana. When Sheryl asked Dr. Simon who was keeping Shana, Ron blurted out something that made her answer inaudible. We later learned that she was with a friend of Dr. Simon. After about thirty minutes or so, the door opened and the rest of us were summoned in to hear the judge's ex-planation of the decision he had made - one that at first pleased us, but in the end upset us greatly. The judge first informed Ron and us that he was not going to let Ron remove Shana from Temple Chris-tian School at the time because that was where her friends were, and she was doing well.

Then he looked at our attorney and said, "If your clients are in-terested in the custody of this child, I suggest you get your petition on file promptly. This child has had enough upheaval in her life. I want to rule on this case as quickly as possible and give her life some stability." Then he added, "If I allow her to be removed from a comfortable setting and placed in a new school now, then hypothetically rule in the Richards' favor, she would be returned to Temple Christian School, and I don't want her to go through that kind of trauma. Starting in about two weeks, I'm going to switch roles giving her father physical custody and the Richards' visitation rights including overnight visitation."

This felt like someone had pounded us in the head with a sledgehammer, and we could only imagine what it would do to Shana.

Our attorney attempted to console us by saying, "I know it's hard but the judge had to give Ron the opportunity to prove what kind of father he can be. We know he'll mess up."

We couldn't have imagined how quickly that prediction would come true - it was already in progress. Ron was obviously upset with the terms of the order, even though he was to be awarded physical custody of Shana. It was to be his responsibility to deliver her to Temple Christian School by 8:30 a.m. and pick her up at 2:30 p.m. This schedule would put a crimp in his life style - he did not like schedules - he wanted to do things when he wanted to. Ron showed his displeasure over the ruling by taking off in a hurry from the courthouse parking area. Perhaps it was the very idea that the judge would even consider the possibility of granting us custody of Shana. He was incensed at the very mention of it and he was determined to prevent it from happening. We did not realize it then, but it would be over four years before we would see Shana again.

What followed seemed like a nightmare from the natural perspective, but was actually a spiritual journey that drew us closer to the Lord than we had ever been before. God was the only one we could count on for comfort and guidance. There is a quotation that says, "When you come to the place where the Lord is all you have, you will find He is all you need." No truer words were ever spoken. Ron did not return Shana from visitation that day, but rather left the area, the state, and eventually the country with her and his mother. He knew his mother's Alzheimer's was the perfect opportunity to gain control of her and her money to finance his flight. He must have been obsessed with a lust for her money, because he constantly bragged about how much she had in her trust account. He estimated it at times to be between $150,000.00 and $300,000.00, but apparently he didn't know for sure - he just knew he wanted it for himself.

We notified our attorney when Shana's father did not return her that day, and even though we didn't know what had happened, Attorney Franklin informed us that we could not file a missing person's report for at least twenty-four hours after her disappearance. Because we knew that Ron could go a long way in that time, we wanted to get a police search started as soon as possible. We were also concerned that Shana would think we had abandoned her even though we were only doing what we were compelled to do. The next day Mr. Franklin advised us to go to the magistrate's office and obtain a felony warrant for parental abduction. We took time off from our jobs and paid the magistrate a visit. As it turned out, he was a fellow that I had attended school and played baseball with.

After we explained our request he asked us a few questions then removed his glasses and slowly commented, "W-e-l-l, it looks to me like if she's with her father, no crime has been committed."

"But it was in violation of the court order," we insisted.

"Well, it looks like the court should pursue it then," he replied as he fumbled with his glasses.

Frustrated, we walked over to the Juvenile and Domestic Relations Court where we informed the clerk of our plight. She managed to contact the judge by phone and after she explained the situation to him, she turned to us again and delivered his response, "The judge says he can't advise you on how to practice law, but suggests you go and see the Commonwealth's Attorney."

Fortunately we found him in his office and were able to share our concerns with him. From there, he accompanied us to the Sheriff's office to give what information we had to the investigator. As Sheryl gave information to the investigator, I ran home to get some pictures and a copy of the court order that gave us joint legal custody with the father. While checking the files, it was discovered that Ron had three Social Security numbers. (Later Craig found two more.) The Social Security Administration has been notified of this and the Internal Revenue Service has been notified of his tax evasion status, but nothing has been done to our knowledge. We also wrote a letter to the Immigration and Naturalization Service about his scheme to smuggle Pakistanis into the United States through Central America and Mexico and got the same results.

When we were finished at the investigator's office, we returned to the Commonwealth Attorney's office and talked some more. He told us, "I will not file a charge against him as a scare tactic and then drop it - if I start it I'm going through with it and you may have to testify in court. It appears you have probable cause to believe a crime has been committed, so if you really want to pursue it I'm ready and willing."

"If that's what it is going to take to get a search started for this little girl then let's get on with it," was our unified response.

After explaining the situation to our attorneys (Ron's and ours) the Commonwealth Attorney headed back to the magistrates office. There he explained to the magistrate that we had probable cause to believe a crime had taken place and that the father might try to leave the state if he had not already.

After the attorney's departure, the magistrate again began fumbling with his glasses and mumbled, "If she's with her father, it doesn't look to me like a crime has been committed unless you can prove he has taken her out of the state."

Even though we were sure Ron would try to take her out of the state of Virginia and even worse - out of the country if not prevented - it was the next day before we could be certain they had indeed left the state. Ron called Craig and told him that he and Shana had left the state, which took Shana out of the jurisdiction of the Amherst County Courts.

"I'm not going to let that county judge tell me what I can and can't do," Craig quoted Ron as saying.

As previously mentioned, Ron characteristically made his moves on weekends or holidays enabling him to get a head start before authorities could act. It was reported that he had studied some law, even though he couldn't pass the bar exam, so he must have had a pretty good idea how law enforcement worked, something we had yet to learn.

That was a dark weekend for us so we requested prayer for Shana through our church - a trend that continued fervently for the next several years. We continued praying for Shana on a regular basis.

Ron evidently figured this was a good time to make his move, since it was Labor Day weekend and most pertinent offices would be closed. It would be Tuesday (approximately four days after his departure), before the magistrate would return to his office. Mr. Franklin had us meet him at the Lynchburg police station where he helped us obtain the necessary warrant.

A few days later Craig informed us that Ron had a hearing scheduled in a New York court concerning the custody of his other two children. I'm not sure if Ron told Craig about the hearing or if Ron's first wife, Annette, had passed it on to him, but at the scheduled time of the hearing, Judge Jacobs contacted the judge in New York who, after hearing about the situation in Virginia, postponed the hearing there and had the New York police take Ron into custody.

About this time, unknown to our attorney and us, Mr. Willard Parker, the Commonwealth's Attorney for Lynchburg had discovered the warrant and decided he did not want to prosecute the case. He had canceled the warrant so that when the New York police checked the computer, the warrant for Ron's arrest for parental abduction had disappeared and they were obligated to release him.

When Mr. Franklin inquired as to why the attorney had done this he replied, "This is a messy case, and I don't want to get involved in it."

His response shocked us, since we did not know this could happen! Apparently prosecuting attorneys can choose to prosecute only the stronger cases that they think they have the best chance of getting a conviction and drop the cases they perceive to be weaker. Also, there seemed to be some controversy as to who should take charge of the investigation - Lynchburg, where the abduction was centered, or Amherst County where the court order was violated. It seemed that neither locality was particularly interested in pursuing it. A subsequent clarification by the Attorney General for the Commonwealth of Virginia indicated that either could or should have since it was now known that Ron had left the state. Our concern was that the longer the authorities hesitated, the better the chance that Ron could secure a passport for Shana and his mother and leave the country.

I have heard the complaint that "laws are designed to help the criminal instead of the victim," but this was our first experience with this type of problem. While we contacted Ron's ex-wife, Annette, in New York for information on potential hiding places, Craig, who held the Power of Attorney for their mother, was able to follow Ron's trail through bills for purchases on their mother's credit card.

Throughout the early portions of this ordeal, we urged the Lynchburg Police investigator to try to prevent Ron from getting a passport for Shana so that he could not take her out of the country, but the investigator said this was next to impossible and tried to assure us that "all was being done that could be done."

"HOGWASH!!"

We discovered eventually that all that needed to be done was to contact the U.S. State Department in Washington, D.C., and inform the Passport Duty Officer what was happening, followed by a fax or certified copy of the court order and he would notify the passport offices, but by then, it was about a week to ten days too late. Ron had managed to get a quickie passport and hustled them all out of the country. We thought the police investigators knew what to do, but apparently they did not.

When we discovered that Ron and Shana had left the country, we were devastated, especially when we were reminded of the conditions under which Shana was last seen. We were concerned that her heart would be broken because we had failed her, but at this point there seemed to be little or nothing we could do except continue to pray. Although we loved her dearly, as if she were our very own, we still had to abide by the laws whether her father did or not. This created quite a bit of turmoil and stress in our lives, but we were fighters so we weren't going to give up. I concluded and assured Sheryl that no one was powerful enough to overthrow God or smart enough to outwit Him (including Ron). It was evident God had a purpose in allowing this to happen or they would never have been able to get out of the country.

Previously I had been convinced that God would not allow this to happen and desired to tell Ron that if he interfered with God's plan for Shana's life, God would eliminate him from the picture completely. However, I was not allowed to do so, because while it seemed like Ron was interfering with God's plan, He was actually carrying out His plan to have Shana placed in our custody permanently. While those who crucified Jesus thought they were doing

God a favor because they didn't know Him, they were actually carrying out His plan for the redemption of mankind (Acts 2:23; 4:28; Ephesians. 1:11).

Likewise when a person who does not know God or His mandate for raising children (Deuteronomy 6:7; 11:19) brings a child into this world who is one of God's elect according to His foreknowledge, (1 Peter 1:2) it is sometimes necessary for God to place them in the custody of someone else so they can be taught the gospel of Jesus Christ and have the opportunity to be saved. This was one of those times. Even though we knew that God's Word is always true including Romans 8:28 ("And we know that all things work together for good to them that love God, to them who are the called according to his purpose"), it was difficult then to understand how this was going to work together for Shana's good or for ours, but we knew it would somehow.

We have since discovered at least four ways in which it has worked together for her good and ours: 1) It tested and strengthened Shana's childlike faith while living in an idolatrous culture (Islam) with no encouragement toward Christianity; 2) It strengthened our faith in God's sovereign rule in the kingdom of men (Proverbs 16:9, 33; Daniel 4:32; Lamentations. 3:37) and drew us closer to Him as we were able to do nothing without Him; 3) It allowed Ron to build a strong case against himself that would assure us future victories; and, 4) It would open several doors for us to witness for our Lord and Savior, Jesus Christ, to many individuals and come to see some of them saved for His glory.

These and other doors are still opening. I earnestly and continually prayed, "Lord, don't let me run ahead of your timing and try to do things on my own. Close the doors if you must, but please help us to be prepared and ready to do what you want us to. In the meantime, keep Shana's faith strong and protect her from harm until you are ready to return her and give us peace in all of this. Amen."

Even though we had committed the situation to the Lord, we were constrained to continue investigating leads personally. We gave the police any information we could come up with, but I got the impression they didn't appreciate our being involved because we kept the pressure on them.

Chapter 8

Meanwhile... Back In The U.S.A.

A week or two after Ron's departure, Attorney Franklin's partner, who specialized in criminal law, suggested that we might garner some clues by consulting a chess magazine or by contacting some chess organization since Ron seemed to like to play chess.

When Sheryl shared this suggestion with some of her coworkers, one lady commented, "My brother plays chess and he gets these chess magazines - I'll call him and see if he can help."

Ron had told us about three Hungarian sisters who were chess prodigies. They were all doing so well in their age groups that their parents allowed them to focus their attention on playing chess rather than continuing their schooling. The oldest at that time was sixteen, (the one Ron propositioned over the telephone) the others about eleven and nine respectively. He had implied that he wanted to manage them and was trying to, or already had, arranged transportation for them on a major airline to an upcoming chess tournament.

When Sheryl's co-worker contacted her brother, he talked to heryl and briefed him on what had happened. Then when she asked him if he knew anything about these three Hungarian sisters, he replied, "Oh yes." Then he proceeded to give their names adding, "They're coached or managed by a man named Ron Simon."

"That's the guy we're looking for," Sheryl quipped.

"Well I'll be doggoned," he said. "I played chess with him in New York just a few weeks ago."

As Sheryl shared a little more information with him he snapped, "Why that 'blankety-blank' rascal!"

Throughout this whole ordeal people asked Sheryl, "How do you keep from going to pieces?"

"I have to stay angry at him to keep my sanity," Sheryl answered.

The Scriptures teach us that God loves the world (John 3:16), but they also tell us that He is angry with the wicked every day (Psalms 7:11). What could be more wicked than calling God a liar? (I John 5:10; Romans 3:4)

A little later the coworker's brother brought Sheryl an issue of the chess magazine. As she scanned through it, guess what she found! There was a chess tournament scheduled in Rio Galagos, Argentina, just a few days hence! Sheryl had me attempt to get some information from the United States Embassy there, but never having made an overseas call before, my attempted calls "could not be completed as dialed." I did not know it then, but one has to dial an overseas code, a country code, a city code, and then the phone number in order to complete a successful call. Later Sheryl tried and was able to get through only to discover that the person on the other end only spoke Spanish. What now?

The next day another coworker said, "I know a couple and the wife is from Argentina. She speaks the language."

After some consultation, Sheryl was able to persuade the wife to place a call and determine if there was indeed a chess match in progress and to find out where the participants were staying.

While there, Ron kept running up his mother's credit card bill. By the time they were ready to check out of the hotel, they had exceeded the limit on her account. Craig refused to use his power of attorney to authorize a transfer of funds from his mother's trust account to cover the bill, so they could not check out of the hotel until it was paid. This is when Ron showed his true colors and sent a fax to the bank, as though it were from his mother, claiming she was revoking Craig's power of attorney. Then he followed it up with a phone call threatening a lawsuit if the bank did not transfer the necessary funds. After some negotiations, and in an effort to avoid a lawsuit, the bank management agreed to provide coverage for them to return to the States.

In the meantime, another one of Sheryl's coworkers told her, "My daughter works for a large travel agency. I'll contact her and see what she can find out about [Ron's] travel plans."

The airline's policy was that no one outside of their employees could enter their computer system unless authorized by one of their employees. It just so happened that this agent's daughter had dated a guy who was an employee of that particular airline and when the request was made, he okayed her to check the schedules. Talk about the hand of God!

After a short time she came across Simon, party of three, departing Buenos Aires. She got the departure time, flight number, and arrival time in Miami. Apparently, the major airlines terminated at Buenos Aires and commuter airlines had taken them to Rio Gallagos and back. Armed with this information, Sheryl contacted the local investigator in Lynchburg and informed him of what she had learned. "Now's your chance to nab him." She said.

He immediately inquired, "Where did you get that information?"

"I'll never tell," she replied, knowing that it might get her co-worker's daughter fired or in serious trouble if she revealed the source.

When it came time for Ron to return to Miami, the police there had been alerted and were to take him into custody, or so we were told. His maternal uncle from Key West was on standby to take Ron's mother under his wing. Sheryl's nephew would be there to keep an eye on Shana if needed until we could arrive to retrieve her. For whatever reason (perhaps Ron was suspicious and he had every right to be, or maybe it was not in his plan from the beginning which is my personal theory) they did not return to Miami.

The next contact we had was a day or two later when Craig received a phone call from his mother, who at that time was in Paris, France. According to Craig, she was sobbing as she said, "I'm tired of traveling and I want to come home. I should not have gone with him. I'll never go anywhere with him again. Can you help me get home?"

"Give me a phone number there and I'll check the schedules and get back to you," Craig replied.

When he did call back, they had checked out of the hotel. Ron knew he had to keep on the move and keep his mother brainwashed if he wanted to keep her under his control. Ron was very overbearing, more verbal than physical, and could talk people into a corner if they weren't careful. This made his mother easy prey, especially in her condition. I've often wondered how he persuaded her to go with him in the first place. Perhaps he persuaded her to spend a little of her savings and see the world. He would be her guide since he was an experienced world traveler, but what he didn't tell her, I'm sure, is that she would have to finance his shenanigans and it would cost her much more than she wanted to spend.

Once Ron got her out of the country he probably told her she would be arrested and charged with abduction if she returned. This is only speculation, of course, but it is reasonable since some taped phone conversations revealed that Ron had been a worry to his mother and was not too well liked by her side of the family. It also caused Craig to develop divided feelings for his mother. Craig said he loved his mother, but it was obvious he was very resentful of the fact that she allowed herself to be duped by Ron.

After Ron took Shana from us, we were busily trying to locate them and hopefully prevent him from taking her out of the country, which we knew he would attempt. One such effort was to have her picture shown on The Old Time Gospel Hour satellite network with a plea for anyone that saw her to notify the police. Another was to have the Real Estate Review print Ron and Shana's pictures on the back of their magazine showing the missing child, her abductor father, and her grandmother as a possible accomplice. Actually, we considered the grandmother a victim while some others thought she voluntarily accompanied him, which could have made her a co-conspirator.

We didn't hear anything more from them for several weeks (maybe months since I didn't keep a diary or log on our contacts) until we got a note from Shana, assisted by her grandmother in one of her clearer moments, I'm sure. Piecing together bits of information from various sources, we were able to determine that they had been through Austria and Hungary, where Shana later said they spent the night with the chess playing family, and then on to Oman and the Persian Gulf before settling temporarily in Abu-Dhabi, capital of the United Arab Emirates.

We responded to Shana's note and asked for a more detailed address so we could send her a birthday present, but we were told there were no street addresses where they were. Actually, it would have made little or no difference if they could have been pinpointed because the United Arab Emirates has no extradition treaty with the U.S.A., therefore, Ron could not be returned to the United States for trial even if Interpol had arrested him.

After a short while, a few months at most, they moved about eighty miles further into the country to a desert town or city named Fujairah and apparently that is where they made their residence for most of the next three and a half or four years, even though Shana claims they lived nearly a year in Sri Lanka at one point. In Abu-Dhabi, she attended an English speaking school where Arabic was also taught. A large segment of Abu-Dhabi's population spoke English and a large English speaking newspaper called the Khaleeji Times was printed there. When they moved to Fujairah, Shana had to attend an Arabic speaking school. Since she had not yet learned to speak Arabic and she said she knew more English than the English teacher, she slept through most of the class. School began very early in the morning and dismissed around noon because of the temperatures above one hundred degrees. It appears Shana received very little formal education between kindergarten and grade four when she returned to the United States.

We eventually received a note from Shana, probably with the help of her grandmother in a clear moment. For the remainder of the next four years, we continued to write to Shana and send packages for her birthday, Christmas, and a new dress for Easter along with presents for Milton and Jinny, her half brother and sister.

Although we continued to pray for Shana's well-being and eventual return we still searched for any way we could be of assistance. Sheryl wrote letters to our senator and congressman to see if they could help. Our senator was concerned about and sympathetic to our plight, and members of his staff remained in close contact throughout his tenure. Our congressman never responded. In addition, we made several requests through the U. S. State Department for information.

During one conversation with the passport duty officer he mentioned that if there was a federal Unlawful Flight to Avoid Prosecution (U. F. A. P.) warrant for Ron, the State Department could revoke Ron's passport. He could now only use it to return to the U.S.A.

We immediately contacted our attorney and our senator. They arranged a conference call along with Sheryl to discuss the situation with a federal judge, who then issued the U. F. A. P. warrant. Sometime after the federal judge issued the U. F. A. P. warrant, the F. B. I. contacted Ron and recommended that he turn himself in, which he eventually did, first in Guam and then in Hawaii. But true to character, Mr. Willard Parker, the Commonwealth's Attorney in Lynchburg, who nol-prossed the warrant and allowed Ron to flee the country with Shana, refused to approve the funds to have him extradited. Initially, he had promised that if Ron would turn himself in anywhere in the United States he would extradite him, but now he changed his tune and said it must be the continental United States.

When Craig and two of his uncles heard about this, they came together and said, "We'll put up the money. You just go and get him."

However, Mr. Parker still refused, saying private financing could not be accepted. He still would not approve state funds. Mr. Parker just did not want Ron.

What I did not mention previously is that the Parker and Simon family ties go way back. Could it be that those ties had anything to do with this and the previous action on Mr. Parker's part which seemed to be in Ron's favor? I suppose only God knows for sure, but it was obvious to us that something was amiss. Eventually, Mr. Parker was compelled to extradite Ron from California when a circuit court judge issued a Capias for his arrest for contempt of court.

Whether the State Department actually revoked his passport, and if so when, I was not informed. Ron seemed to be able to travel at will for at least the first two or three years after he left the United States with Shana. Sheryl also informed the State Department that she had seen two passports for Ron, one in his birth name and one in his adopted Muslim name, which the State Department said was a felony, but he continued to use them alternately for some time.

In the middle of this turmoil, Sheryl and I flew to Germany in

1987 to visit our son Landen, a member of the United States Air Force, and his family, who were stationed there. A few months after our return from Germany, I got fed up with my company's bonus system, which had essentially transformed my department into a slave shop, so I changed jobs. Ron somehow found out that I was no longer employed there. He told Shana that I had been fired, which was definitely a lie.

The following year, 1988, the interior of our house was damaged by fire. Our home had to be completely re-done, including appliances, most furniture, and clothes. The basic structure was undamaged. Most of the fire damage was limited to the kitchen and dining area from about three to four feet upward because the fire had about burned itself out for lack of oxygen by the time the fire department arrived. Smoke and soot was spread throughout the house by the air conditioner. About a quart of water was required to extinguish some papers, which had been left in an antique wooden salad bowl. I remember the fire occurred on a Wednesday afternoon. Sheryl was at work and I had either taken off from work or was on vacation at the time. We went to church that night with the clothes on our backs.

Needless to say, the hectic conditions under which we were struggling because of the house fire made some items such as addresses and writing materials hard to locate. We did not write to Shana as often as we would have liked, especially around Thanksgiving, but we had a lot to be thankful for. We had been out of our home since August 9, 1988, but were able to move back in December 10, 1988, just in time to get settled for Christmas.

When we wrote Shana that we were back in our "new" house and sent her pictures of our new furnishings, it upset Ron terribly. He apparently hoped we had lost everything. Even though most of our appliances were twenty-four years old and were still working, the Lord felt they needed to be replaced, I suppose. I must admit that some of the new ones don't work as well as the old ones did.

As time went on we wished we had taught Shana to use the telephone, but we gradually realized it would have been futile because Shana was only four years and nine months old when Ron abducted her from us. It seemed that our hands were tied after they settled down in the U. A. E., but we could still pray and that we did. Also, part of our phone number had changed so we eventually wrote Sha-na a letter telling her how much we loved her, missed seeing her, and hearing the sound of her voice. We invited her to call us anytime. I didn't know the procedure for reaching the operator in the U. A. E., but I figured someone there could help her with that.

"Just tell the operator you want to make a collect call to the United States of America and give her our phone number," which we included.

Chapter 9

Legal Battles Begin

Soon after settling down in the United Arab Emirates, Ron, impersonating his mother by mail, again tried to convince the bank, that held her money that she had revoked Craig's power of attorney and given it to Ron in an effort to force/persuade them to transfer her assets to his control.

Beginning sometime in 1988 or early 1989 we were faced with the first of many lawsuits, appeals, petitions, etc. There were about fourteen in all, which continued for the next five or six years. To prevent Ron from getting his mother's savings transferred to the United Arab Emirates where he could plunder it, Craig and his uncle arranged for a hearing before a circuit court judge in Lynchburg, Virginia, where they presented records from Duke University that proved that Dr. Simon's diagnosis preceded the supposed revocation of the original power of attorney given to Craig.

The decision was that any subsequent action allegedly taken by Dr. Simon was suspect unless she returned to the States to prove otherwise so the judge froze her trust account and ruled the original power of attorney, still valid and any newer one (if one existed) invalid. Of course, Ron could not allow his mother to return lest her condition be confirmed and his forgeries be revealed. We knew these actions were his and not his mother's as he claimed. Since he considered us to be allied with his family against him, he included us along with his brother, uncle, our respective attorneys, Lynchburg's Commonwealth's Attorney, (Mr. Willard Parker), the bank that held his mother's trust account, their attorneys, and several others in a five million dollar lawsuit. That lawsuit was followed later by a ten million dollar suit and then yet another one for twenty-five thousand dollars. Some specific allegations have become hazy in my mind, due to the rising onslaught and the passing of time, but all of them seemed to center primarily on the claim that we had conspired to steal his mother's money and kidnap her granddaughter, portraying his mother as the accuser.

It was obvious that Ron was obsessed with his mother's money because he made mention of it in all of his lawsuits, sometimes more than once. As for kidnapping his daughter, he was the only one who did that. We desired to prevent him from doing so and were trying to have her returned to the jurisdiction of the court from which he had taken her, concluding that no judge in his right mind would place her in Ron's custody after he had fled with her.

I developed a theory about Ron that I called in layman's language a 'reverse psychological disorder' or 'mirror image.' While the allegations against others were preposterous, they described him almost perfectly. The actions he accused of others were exactly what he had done or was trying to do. It was as if he were trying to frame someone else to divert attention from himself, but his actions were so obvious that few people, who knew anything at all about him, were fooled by it.

During these proceedings in the Lynchburg Circuit Court, the judge and Commonwealth's Attorney were represented by a lady from the Attorney General's office in Richmond, Virginia. Another lady attorney, who we later learned was our attorney's part time assistant was representing our attorney. Since our attorney was also a defendant and therefore represented by another attorney, that left us without any legal representation. Ron's uncle was also on his own. But what the heck!? If the 'big peas in the pod' were successfully defended, the little peas (us) would hardly be noticed we figured - and we were right.

When the presiding judge looked over the list of allegations, he looked up and asked, "Where are the litigants? Are they in the courtroom?"

"No, your honor," was the reply from the attorneys.

"Don't they know they have to be here in person to litigate these charges?" He then appointed one of the attorneys to thus inform Ron and his mother and postponed the hearing until such a time as they could be present. The case was later dismissed for lack of a response. The other lawsuits were handled in a similar fashion.

As we filed out of the courtroom I asked Mr. Parker, "Why do you suppose Ron is suing you? It seems you did him a big favor when you turned him loose and allowed him to get out of the country."

I intended for the latter part of the question to be a little sarcastic, but I made it sound as if I were seriously inquisitive so as not to rattle him too much.

"Just because he knows my name I guess," he replied.

Meanwhile Sheryl was being approached by the lady assistant, who was representing our attorney, for more information on Ron's second abduction of Shana and the time between the two abductions when Shana was in our care. Being a mother of two young girls herself, the attorney was very sympathetic towards our plight. She confided in Sheryl that she felt Shana should be in our custody. She would later become our attorney and put together a solid case (which Ron had basically built against himself) to accomplish this goal.

Chapter 10

Escape Planning

While planning for our 1989 vacation, Sheryl and I decided to investigate the possibility of renting the Simon family's apartment at Myrtle Beach, South Carolina. We called Craig and asked him if he thought his widowed aunt would rent it to us.

After Craig had contacted her, he called Sheryl back and said that no his aunt would not rent it to us, but we could use it for free and told us how to go about getting the key. We were soon on our way. The apartment was a rather small addition to the side of a house they owned and rented out. It was adequate for the two of us, and we were blessed to be able to use it, but we sure missed Shana knowing how much she loved the beach.

After a couple of days, it began to rain lightly and the temperature turned cooler, so we decided to pull out and spend the rest of our vacation somewhere else. Although it was still cloudy and cool when we left, the rain did let up enough that we were able to take a few snapshots. One was of me standing atop a pile of rocks. We eventually sent the photo to Shana and it ended up surfacing a little over a year later, you will see, in a most unusual place.

Sheryl decided she wanted to go to Lancaster and Reading, Pennsylvania and shop at the outlet stores. We decided that since we would be passing so close to home it made more sense to spend the night there and leave again the next morning rather than to spend the night on the road in a motel.

About 4:30 a.m. (12:30 p.m. U. A. E. time), we were awakened by the telephone ringing. When Sheryl roused enough to answer it, there was a pause after the hello. I couldn't hear what was coming over the phone.

Then in an exited tone, Sheryl said, "Shana, is that you? How are you sweetheart? It's so good to hear your voice!"

Shortly, another voice came on the line and sounded so much like Shana that Sheryl was frequently asking, "Who am I talking to now?"

It was Oshia, one of Ron's Sri Lankan wives, mother of Jinny. She spoke fairly good English with an accent, but sounded as young as Shana. Since Shana had picked up some of the same accent over the past three years, it was difficult to tell them apart. Oshia said she had written us a letter asking for help in getting away from Ron because he was not good to her and wanted know if we had received it yet.

Sheryl responded, "I don't know if we can help you get away from him or not, but if you can help us get Shana back we'll do whatever we can."

Obviously, Shana had confided in Oshia about her abduction and they had become close like sisters. When Oshia got ticked off at Ron, she wanted to retaliate by escorting Shana back to the States. This process took a little over a year of planning and scheming before a door finally opened that would allow it to become a reality. We were given their phone number, but were advised not to call there because they didn't want Ron to get suspicious. They would call us collect when he was away. Sometimes when he would come home unexpectedly, they would abruptly hang up. Either they were super deceivers or Ron wasn't as smart as he thought he was because according to them "he never suspected a thing."

There were two major hurdles Oshia had to overcome, and I couldn't be much help to her. The first was that she needed a visa to enter the United States since she was not a U. S. citizen. The second was that Ron kept their passports locked in a safe deposit box. One scheme Oshia suggested was that she would try to persuade Ron to let Shana go with her to visit her home (Sri Lanka) while I would try to persuade the consular officer in Colombo (Sri Lanka) to grant her a visa. Once they were ready to leave for Sri Lanka, I was to fly there to meet them. If Oshia couldn't get a visa, I could bring Shana back to the States myself.

For some reason, this plan never did materialize, even though Oshia said Ron had agreed for her to go. I don't know just what the glitch was, whether he would not buy her a ticket or what, but I think it was God's timing. The plan was rather risky anyway and I didn't want Oshia to get into any trouble.

I continued to pray as I always had, "Lord, please don't let me run ahead of you and try to do things on my own, but do help me to be wise enough to act at your bidding."

I was anxious for things to happen and was convinced God would bring Shana back, but if any plan would work it would have to be His. I knew that I couldn't accomplish anything on my own.

I understood one must have an Arab sponsor to enter the U. A. E., and I was searching for one of those in case I needed to go there. I guess I was foolish enough to think that the U. S. State Department would take Shana into custody, and I could pick her up since Ron had taken her in violation of a court order, but this was not the case. I finally realized that the State Department's responsibility was not to settle legal disputes between U. S. citizens even if one of them may have committed a crime, but rather to represent them if they ran into problems in a foreign country.

Oshia expressed the desire to have a friend accompany her to the U.S., but this idea created more problems because the embassies were apparently suspicious and reluctant to grant either of them a visa. I did what I could to persuade the embassies, but to no avail, which was probably best because it could have opened up a whole keg of worms with the Immigration and Naturalization Service if both of them came and then didn't want to return after a visit. Ron claimed Oshia was his wife and she was the mother of a U.S. citizen, Jinny, one of Ron's children. All of Ron's children were born in the U.S., including those conceived in the U. A. E. He had told Oshia that this was done so he could put them on welfare and make a living that way. This comment was made by a man who had paid little or nothing in the way of social security or income taxes.

I was later told by one of the Catholic nuns in California, that Ron had dropped Oshia off in San Francisco where she was to contact the Catholic charities with some sad plea for help. She was Catholic at the time, so the nuns took her in and provided for her during the latter part of her pregnancy and delivery. When she and the baby were able to travel, Ron returned and hustled them away without paying the bill the same as he had done with Dorothy, his third wife and her son, Milton. The Catholics contemplated filing a suit against him, but apparently never followed through with it. They either figured it would cost more money than they could actually recover or they were ashamed to admit they had been duped twice by the same guy.

Nothing seemed to be clicking as far as getting Shana back to us in 1989, but we were still able to talk to her and we were thankful for that. Oshia said that Shana would cry nearly every day saying, "I want to see my mommy before Christmas."

Our hearts were still broken, but we were comforted by the fact that we were able to hear her voice. The calls kept coming - sometimes once every two or three weeks, sometimes two or three times a week. Our son, Landen was in the U.S. Air Force and he and his family were still stationed in Germany. Sheryl preferred to talk to them on the phone rather than write, so our phone bills were quite high. They averaged $300 to $500 per month and one was over $700! I gently hinted to Shana and Oshia that they space the calls out a little, especially when there were no new developments. We enjoyed hearing from them, but needed to conserve finances for the time when things would start popping and we didn't know when that would be.

We continued to pray, but now with a little more intensity. I was impressed to lay it on the line before God and to tell Him exactly how I felt. No one has the authority to tell God what to do or the power to persuade Him to do it. Therefore, many of His children act like wimps, afraid to level with Him for fear of being chastised even though He has invited His children to "come boldly to the throne of grace that we may obtain mercy, and find grace to help in time of need" (Hebrews 4:16). God may not give us what we ask for when we ask for it. He may give us grace to help us until the time - His timing - is right, but He always gives us what we need, when we need it, if we humble ourselves before Him.

Moses was able to reason with God because he had a close walk with Him (Exodus 32:11-14,32), much closer than I. Though God had called him to lead His people out of Egypt and into the promised land, Moses was as human as you and I - as were the other apostles and prophets. (Acts 14:15, James 5:17)

God promised in Jeremiah 33:3 (my favorite prayer verse): "Call unto me and I will answer thee and show thee great and mighty things which thou knowest not."

Bolstered by these and other Scriptures, I began to pray, "Oh Father, you promised if we would call unto you that you would answer us and especially if we ask anything according to your will (1 John 5:14). Lord, I know it was your will for this child to be saved (1 Timothy 2:4) and she was. I'm not asking for my sake that you return her safe and sound (in the faith), but for her sake (James 4:3) because she will get no encouragement from her father who claims to be a Muslim and is against your son, Jesus (Matthew 12:30). Also, you firmly declare that you are more loving and compassionate than any earthly father (Luke 11:11-13; John 14:21-23, 15:7). Father, I'm not trying to alter your timetable - I just want to hear from you. If I had bombarded my earthly father when he was alive as I have you, I believe he would have answered by now, even if he said nothing but 'shut up and leave me alone!' Oh, Heavenly Father, please don't disappoint me. I need an answer from you soon. Actions can come later if they must."

Often times we ask for things that are according to His will, but because of our lack of faith He delays answering and we begin to doubt, but that is our mistake. We need to be persistent (Matthew 7:7,8; 21:22, Mark 11:24, Luke 11:9,10). I never doubted that God would return Shana to our trust so that she might be nurtured by His word. I just didn't know when and must confess, I was getting a little impatient.

Our choir at Temple Baptist Church sings a song occasionally that I dearly love. The chorus says something about God being always on time. Even if things don't happen when we think they should, God is always on time.

Chapter 11

The Great Escape

One day in August or September of 1990, we got a call from Craig informing us that Ron, his mother, and his children were in Bangkok, Thailand, and that this might be our best chance of getting Shana back. The U. A. E. had an Islamic government and by their law children are the property of the fathers; therefore, mothers have no custody rights. The Islamics are strict on those who disagree. As you are probably aware, Muslims (especially militants) refer to the U. S. as the Great Satan and do not recognize or honor our laws. Thailand, on the other hand, is more democratic like America except that their major religion is Buddhism.

We found out later that Ron had sent Dorothy to the U. S. to have another baby, but this time to New York. He probably hoped that Catholic charities there didn't find out about his little scheme in California.

Also, by this time Oshia had left Jinny with Ron and gone back to Sri Lanka to supposedly get married. Oshia later told us that while Ron had signed some kind of marriage certificate to get her out of her country, they were never legally married. She also told a gruesome tale of how he drugged her and raped her, which she later recanted in court, so I don't know how much, if any of it, is true. Obviously, she very much resented the way he had treated her judging by the contents of her letter the year before.

With both of his wives gone (Dorothy to New York - Oshia to Sri Lanka) Ron rounded up his mother (now in her late 70's), Shana (age 8), Milton and Jinny (both 2 years of age) and set out in search of more domestic help. His intended destination was the Philippines, but he was barred from entry and was forced to continue to the next stop, which was Bangkok, Thailand. It was here that his ailing mother was hospitalized with pneumonia. According to Craig, his mother had carried an insurance policy that would have covered her while traveling outside of the United States, but for some reason it was allowed to lapse. Just whose responsibility it should have been to pay the premiums would be hard to determine due to the controversy over who had the power of attorney for their mother. It is believed that a neutral bank was appointed to be responsible for guarding her trust account until the dispute was settled thus tying Craig's hands.

Ron, on the other hand, was controlling her Social Security and retirement pension so probably could have kept up the premiums if he wanted to. The result was that they needed money to pay for her hospital stay so Ron contacted the U. S. Embassy in Bangkok for help. The embassy relayed the request to the U. S. State Department in Washington D.C., and the State Department contacted Craig for a solution.

After contacting his uncles on his mother's side, they agreed to provide the necessary funds themselves only when Dr. Simon was released in their custody. This plan may have been devised after Craig first flew to Bangkok and met with the U.S. Embassy personnel, with whom he was acquainted. They recommended that he engage a Thai attorney who advised him, "I know you want to see your mother, but it would be best for you not to go where Ron is and stir things up for now. Return home and round up the necessary paper work (prior court decisions, notarized Power of Attorney transfer, etc.) so we can represent you here."

I was taking a week's vacation about that time and Sheryl and I were camping at a nearby lake, but I spent several days running back and forth to Lynchburg where I secured the information Craig requested and mailed it to him. Craig mailed these documents to his uncle who lived near Washington, D.C., who in turn took them to Richmond, Virginia, to be authenticated by the Secretary of the Commonwealth of Virginia then back to Washington, D.C. to be authenticated by the U. S. State Department, and on to the Thai Embassy for the same procedure. Then and only then could the information be introduced in the Thai courts as legal documents.

Shortly thereafter, I would follow the same procedure so that this same law firm could represent us. With all the necessary authorization in hand, the Thai lawyer approached Ron and informed him that he now had the authority to decide what happened to Dr. Simon instead of Craig, and that if Craig interfered, he would be jailed.

About this time Oshia (apparently feeling guilty about leaving her daughter behind) returned to the U. A. E. where they had been living only to find Ron, his mother, Shana, Milton, and Jinny all gone and none of those remaining knew where they went. I was surprised when I received a frantic call from her wanting to know if I knew where they were.

Since my wife had previously warned me, "Don't let that woman talk you into anything." I was cautious, suspicious that maybe it was someone else fishing for information since I could not identify people whom I had never met solely by their voice. After quizzing her for a few minutes, I was convinced she was who she said she was and gave her the information I had: the name of the hospital, telephone number, room number, law firm, etc., even though it was risky to trust a total stranger.

Oshia placed a phone call to the hospital room and talked to Shana, who was the primary, if not sole baby sitter for Milton and Jinny. She found out they had stayed in the hospital room with their grandmother for several weeks sleeping on the floor, and she said the two younger ones were fighting over a scrap of bread. The American investigator, who was working for the Thai lawyer, informed me that the children were without adequate supervision and that Milton had been rescued at least once from a precarious perch atop a balcony railing to prevent him from falling into the parking lot below.

He was also concerned about what would happen to the children if the Thai Department of Child Welfare or its equivalent placed them in custodial care since neither of their mothers were on hand to care for them. The Thai law firm was now representing us and was in the process of arranging an emergency hearing to gain custody of Shana so she could be returned to the U. S. Even though a supplemental court order in Virginia had replaced the previous one that would have given her father physical custody and officially placed her in the custody of the Social Services in Amherst County, we were authorized to fly to Bangkok and escort her back if she were in fact taken into custody. The Thai court did hand down the order for custody of Shana, but because of some intermediate developments they were not able to serve Ron with the order because he had again escaped.

Apparently Oshia called the investigator after calling the hospital to inform them she was the mother of one of the children and was coming to retrieve her daughter. She was advised not to come without obtaining a visa first or she would not be allowed to enter the country. She borrowed some money from a friend and in haste set out for Bangkok ignoring the advice. The next time I heard from her was when I received a collect call for help from the airport where she was being held in the customs area because she did not have a visa. I told her that I could not be of any help to her there, but I would call the investigator and see if he could help her. This was late Saturday evening or early Sunday morning.

The investigator's first reaction to my call was to utter a few choice curse words, which was customary for him followed by, "I told her not to come without a visa." He relented and said they would attempt to locate her even though it would be difficult.

The lawyers in Bangkok were successful in finding Oshia after a while. Thinking she would be of help to our side of the case, they scraped together what money they had and borrowed the rest from the Thai police to purchase a round trip ticket to Singapore to obtain a visa. Then they added another $2,000 to my bill.

Just prior to Ron's departure from Thailand, an uncle and a cousin arrived in Bangkok. A lawyer, his staff, and police were able to slip Dr. Simon out of her hospital room and put her on a flight with her relatives back to the States. Since that took away Ron's meal ticket, he would certainly have to return to the U.S. to fight it.

Also about this time I received a step-by-step plan for Shana's recovery and what each phase would cost, the last being when she was released to our custody with a final bill of $50,000. That's when I got on the phone and told them, "Hold everything." I told them I was not wealthy and did not have that kind of money, and if that was what it was going to cost, they would have to discontinue their services immediately. I had already paid them $10,000 for their investment and time in court plus $2,000 for Oshia's round trip to Singapore to obtain a visa.

After I told them I didn't have the money, they revealed that Ron had eluded them and there was nothing more they could do unless they could locate him. Ron must have sensed he was being targeted for allowing the children to run free in a big city without adequate supervision or perhaps that the attorney was seeking custody of Shana because he locked the children in a hotel room for a day or two then left them with someone in a remote area some distance from Bangkok. A rare coincidence allowed Ron and Oshia to find each other at a public phone bank where he talked her into helping him escape with the children.

According to her, they took an all night bus trip, retrieving the children and arriving at the southern tip of Thailand where he bribed a border guard and crossed the border into Malaysia. From there they were able to get a flight back to the U. A. E.

About two days later, Oshia called and said, "We're back in the U. A. E., but Ron is in jail. I have a visa and passports in my possession. All I need is tickets."

"Let me check with the travel agency and I will get back to you with the schedule," I responded.

"We're almost out of food and they're going to cut off the phone," she lamented and gave me another phone number where they would be staying.

Since we began planning the escape in 1989, we had a local travel agency on notice so that when the time was right they could arrange prepaid tickets to Trans World Airline's offices in Abu Dhabi by computer in a matter of a few minutes. By this time, our son Jake was working for the travel agency because the commuter airlines he had worked for closed their office in Lynchburg and he chose not to relocate. Also, the travel agency used the same computer system he had used to make reservations for the airline, so when I called they put him on the case.

This was near the middle of the week and the first confirmed reservation available was the following Monday. The reservations were set-up so they could not be cashed in and, as with all airline tickets, they were non-transferable and would have to be used by those in whose names they were reserved or we would not be charged. Other Service Information remarks were carefully documented in the reservation to explain to the airline that Oshia was assisting with the return of an abducted child.

When we first discussed the tickets, Oshia only wanted tickets for herself, Jinny and, Shana. Being aware that she was expected to be responsible for Milton, I asked her what she was going to do with him.

"I'll leave him with a friend," she said.

A short time after Oshia called and told me that she had the visa and passports. They had their suitcase packed and were out on the street to catch a taxi when who came in sight, but Ron. Apparently, the police had released him sooner than expected.

"Quick, Shana, hide the suitcase while I stall him!" Insisted Oshia.

Poor little Shana, a spindly 8 year old, had to lug the heavy suitcase up the porch stairs into the house, and hide it under the bed while Oshia involved Ron in conversation. Apparently she was about as deceptive as he was.

"We have been invited to a wedding party and we want to go," she explained.

"Okay, but you'll have to take Milton with you," he insisted. "I'm tired and need to rest."

While he slept, they left for the USA! Shana left behind a note saying, "Don't worry we'll be back," with a telephone number to reach them. She told us that Oshia got the number from a pay telephone.

When they did not return that night, Ron became only a little concerned since he had heard on the television or radio that some important figure had died. As is the custom sometimes, the whole country goes into mourning and most businesses close down including public transportation. He surmised that was why they had not come home. He did get concerned when the telephone number he was given turned out to be a phony.

Apparently they had planned to spend the night at one place and keep on the move so they would be harder to locate, because when I called Friday at the number they had given me they had gone to another location and left another number. When I called that number, the call did not go through, so I called the previous number again and tried to explain my problem to the man who answered, but he did not speak good English and I had a hard time understanding him. I finally managed to get the message, "Call back tomorrow and my wife will be here and she can tell you how to contact them."

I was more than a little concerned by now because the reservations were for Monday morning. When I called back Saturday, I spoke with this man's wife who spoke much better English. I explained to her that I couldn't reach Oshia and the children. She asked, "What number did you use?"

When I read it to her, she exclaimed, "Oh, they're in another city now; they're in Abu-Dhabi."

I had forgotten to use the city code for Abu-Dhabi and had used the one for Fujairah instead.

It was such a relief when I finally reached them, whew! I asked Shana if she had a piece of paper and pencil and I gave her all of the information in regards to the airline, flight number, time of departure, routing, layover in London, arrival time, etc., and wished them luck with a request to call me from London so we could prepare to pick them up at Washington National Airport.

I was concerned throughout the planning phase that Oshia might be apprehended and charged with abducting Jinny from the U. A. E. if Ron suspected what they were up to. She assured me she would be okay and God made it so.

Before they left, Oshia contacted an acquaintance in Abu Dhabi who was looking for a housemaid and told him she would no longer be needing hers (she didn't even have one) and asked if they could spend the night. She promised to go and bring the housemaid back to meet him the next morning, to which he apparently agreed. The next morning they left Milton sleeping while they supposedly went to get the housemaid, but instead took a taxi to the airport. It is not clear how they got the suitcase out of the house without the man getting suspicious or whether they had hidden it somewhere the night before.

When they arrived at the airport Oshia had Shana wait outside while she picked up the tickets so they wouldn't be seen together in case someone was looking for them.

When she returned she asked Shana, "Where is the suitcase?"

"What suitcase?" Shana responded. She had forgotten to get it out of the taxi and the driver had driven off with it! Everything they had was in that suitcase except what they had on, and of course the passports and visa, which Oshia had put in her handbag. Without the passports and visas they would have been stuck. It was the providence of God! After they boarded the flight and were ready to get underway, they told me they jumped up and down and shouted excitedly, "We did it! We did it!"

When the man who needed the housemaid, discovered Oshia and Shana were not returning with the housemaid for Milton, he called the police and reported what had happened. Meanwhile, Ron had become suspicious and had also contacted the police. As a result, he and Milton were reunited.

I had instructed Oshia to call me from London to let me know they were on their way so we could prepare to meet them. You can imagine my excitement when my phone rang with a collect call from the United Kingdom! I was working outside with my cordless phone nearby so I would hear when she called.

After a brief, excited exchange, I reminded her not to get off at Kennedy Airport in New York, their first U.S. stop, but to continue on to the Washington National Airport in D.C., where we would meet them. The flight was scheduled to arrive at 12:20 a.m. Oshia inquired about how she would recognize me, and we exchanged information about our descriptions. I had seen a picture of her and knew she would be dark complexioned with a two year old child and, of course, Shana, whom we thought we could recognize even though we hadn't seen her for four years.

Because I couldn't contain my excitement, I called Sheryl at work and shared the good news with her. I think she accepted the fact that they were actually on their way, even though she had not previously been as optimistic as I had, that this plan was actually going to work or maybe she was concerned about what to do next after they arrived. I was on cloud nine to say the least because I had fully committed this situation to the Lord and was fully persuaded that He was answering our prayers at last! Praise God!

We had requested prayers for them from our fellow church members regularly for the past four years. Our fall revival services were starting that very night, Monday, October 7 (or 8th) of 1990. I called our church secretary and requested prayer again.

Since Sheryl and I were too excited to eat before we left, we left early enough to stop and eat along the way. We were so excited! We were almost ecstatic as we made our way to Washington DC, not realizing until later, what a narrow escape Oshia and Shana had in London. You can imagine the suspicions of the customs officials, seeing this young lady who appeared to be about sixteen years old, although she was actually twenty-two, traveling with a two year old in her arms as well as an eight year old nearly half way around the world with no luggage, only the clothes on their backs, having left their suitcase in the taxi in Abu Dhabi. The customs agents, in fact, were so suspicious, that Oshia was herded into a private room where she was strip-searched for contraband. They were inclined, she said, to send them back to the U.A.E., but relented after she convinced them that her husband was a wealthy American and that they were going to visit his family in America.

We arrived at the airport about an hour early so we could find a good parking place and familiarize ourselves with the layout. Then we waited anxiously. There was no question that we were wound up and hyper while we waited. We would sit a little while, get up and walk around, then sit a little longer, then get up and walk around some more. Obviously, we did not want to go to sleep while waiting.

Finally the airlines announced the arrival of their flight, and we were on our feet as we watched the passengers file into the terminal. When it looked like all of them were in and there was no sight of Shana, Oshia, or Jinny, our hearts sank and a queasy, sickening feeling began to grip our stomachs as we wondered what could have happened.

Just then Sheryl exclaimed, "Wait, I think I see a small child at the other end of the hall!"

We prayed as they slowly approached. Sure enough, it was them and the moment we had waited for! Shana had fallen asleep and had to be awakened. Then they had to search for one of Jinny's shoes that was lost. Add that to the fact that they were tired from their long journey, plus they had lost everything they owned. It was understandable why they weren't very energetic.

They were a little shy and not too talkative at first, but when we all got into the car and headed for home, they gradually began to open up a little. Then we stopped briefly to eat something along the way. We stopped somewhere closer to home to get diapers for Jinny as she was in need of a change.

We finally arrived home around 5:30 a.m. and we shared the good news with Craig and his family that Shana was back with us. Then we called the home of some of our close friends from church and shared it with them and from there the news spread. The friends we contacted from the church asked us about our schedule for the day, and Sheryl replied that we were going to get some shut-eye for two to three hours and then were going shopping for some clothes because of the lost suitcase. They asked us to make our first stop at their house. After a couple of hours or so, we were still too excited to sleep so we went ahead to our friends' home to visit. They brought out some clothes that their daughter, who was now in college, had outgrown. Sheryl found some that would fit Oshia. Then they gave us $200 to shop for some more.

That night, after I had gone to work, the others went to our church revival service where everyone gave God thanks and praise for answered prayer. The following night they attended again and this time Oshia made a profession of faith in Jesus Christ as her Lord and Savior. For the first time, I began to realize why God allowed this to happen. Here was a small child, taken nearly half way around the world. On her journey God planned for her to meet and befriend a stranger. She eventually returned with her to the United States where this friend would hear the Gospel of Jesus Christ (Romans 1:16) as she'd probably never heard it before and be persuaded to receive Him as her Lord and Savior. I'm very well aware that God could have handled this situation in a number of different ways without us, but He had been setting the stage for several years. Who am I to question the sovereignty of God? This situation has given me many opportunities to witness for God for which I give Him all the glory.

We called our attorney and asked him if he would still represent us now that Shana was back. He went ahead and assigned his assistant, Lana Davis, to our case. She was the same lady who had defended Attorney Franklin in the earlier lawsuit. The first thing she did was file a petition for the custody of Shana on our behalf. We had filed one in 1986 at the judge's suggestion, but Ron was already out of the country or at least well on his way. We then called Social Services and informed them that Shana had returned. A couple of the social workers came to our house and after a brief inquiry designated us as Shana's foster parents. I assured them that I was not concerned about money and have never been paid any.

A couple of days later, I received a call from an employee of the U.S. State Department stating that Ron claimed someone had kidnapped his children. Naturally, he blamed us.

The employee asked us, "Do you have any idea where they are?"

"Yes, they are here with us safe and sound." We assured her.

"Good. He also claims that someone has taken his passport and it would take several days to get a new one. Do you know anything about that?" She inquired.

Not wanting to reveal immediately what Shana and Oshia had told me, I responded, "I think they hid it."

"They should have burned it," the employee quipped.

Determining that she was more of an ally than an enemy, I told her what Shana and Oshia had told me.

"They told me they threw it in a sewer pit. I don't think he'd want to use it even if he could find it."

"Ha, Ha, goody, goody!" Was her elated response.

They had apparently had enough of him.

After Oshia's profession of faith in Jesus, she was very inquisitive about the Bible, which was good. We tried to satisfy her curiosity by answering as many questions as possible. We had difficulty convincing her that it would take time to learn everything she wanted to know about the Bible. Later we were able to obtain a Bible in her native language of Singhalese through the Gideons, only to discover she couldn't read it. She said her father was killed in the military when she was only eight years old, and since education was not a priority for girls in her country, most, if not all, of the family's education budget was spent on her brother.

One night after dinner we were all sitting around the dining room table, which was a popular place for the family to gather, I read about the births of Ishmael and Isaac to Abraham. I read about the rejection of Ishmael and the acceptance of Isaac as the promised seed through which the Messiah would come (Genesis 21:9-12). Then I compared the prophecy concerning Ishmael's character (Genesis 16:12) to that of Ron whose adopted Muslim name was pronounced and spelled almost identically. As I was attempting to explain Ishmael as being the head of the Arab race as Isaac and Jacob were of the Jewish race and what I thought I knew about their respective religious beliefs, Shana took over and it soon became apparent that she had learned a lot more about Islam than I. She began explaining what the Muslims believe.

Soon Oshia asked, "Do you really believe that?"

Shana shook her head, and nonchalantly replied, "Nope."

Ron had previously told me that Muslims re-tell the story of Ishmael and Isaac to indicate that Ishmael was the promised seed instead of Isaac. Satan is still up to his old tricks (Genesis 3:4,5; John 8:44). We had prayed earnestly that God would protect Shana's faith and not allow her to be influenced by false religion or suffer psychological scars from it, and God was faithful in granting our request.

On more than one occasion, according to Shana's account, she backed Ron into a corner by asking him questions he couldn't answer. She was pretty sharp for an eight year old! One of these was when he was trying to convince Shana that she should be a Muslim. I understand that one of his parents was a Methodist and the other an Episcopalian. Though it doesn't prove they were born-again Christians, Ron's parents at least professed to be Christians.

Shana responded to his pressure by asking, "If I'm supposed to become a Muslim because you and my mother are Muslim, then how come you aren't a Christian if your mother and father claim to be Christians?"

Ron had no answer.

On another occasion while they were dining in another country, Ron was enjoying pork in one form or another when Shana asked,

"How come you're eating pork when Muslims are not supposed to eat pork?"

Ron sheepishly replied, "Because I can get away with it here."

Obviously Shana could not be a Muslim because she dearly loves bacon and more importantly she had received Jesus Christ as her Lord and Savior, an eternal decision.

One may jump from religion to religion even claiming to be a Christian, but once he has been truly born again (John 1:11-13, 3:5-7) and locked into the truth (John 14:6; Ephesians 4:21) he has been sealed by the Holy Spirit (Ephesians 4:30) and cannot lose that salvation (John 5:24, I John 5:13).

Chapter 12

Legal Battles Continue

What transpired over the next five years was like a nightmare and could have been a disaster had God not been in control. Legal battles can be like a spider web to a fly when you don't understand much about how court cases are conducted, and especially when facing outright lies, false allegations, half-truths, and distortions of fact hurled at us by Ron. Fortunately, God provided a Christian attorney to represent us. Ron hurt himself more than he did us by some of his ridiculous and outlandish accusations, which were too far fetched for anyone in their right mind to believe.

When Ron obtained replacement passports after a few weeks, he and Milton came back to America. After making contact with Milton's mother, Dorothy, in New York, Ron and Milton continued on to Amherst, Virginia, where he called Social Services and informed them he was coming to reclaim his daughter, Shana. When he arrived at the Social Services office, he was greeted by a senior caseworker, Mr. Rodger Grimes, who had placed Shana in our foster care. After a period of conversation during which Mr. Grimes listened to some of Ron's complaints against Social Services, Judge Jacobs, and us, Mr. Grimes stepped out of his office. Upon his return he was accompanied by the Amherst County Sheriff, who promptly arrested Ron on an order signed by Judge Jacobs because of the 1986 abduction. Ron's attorney managed to successfully appeal to a circuit court judge and have the bond lowered so that after a few days he was released.

In the meantime, however, Dorothy was upset because Ron did

not leave Milton with her in New York. She was staying at a shelter for abused women operated by a pastor and his wife from Community Bible Church. Dorothy had our telephone number because Oshia had called her from our home; she had the pastor's wife call me to find out where Milton was. When I told her what I knew, she was very upset because Milton was in the care of a stranger. She contacted the Amherst Sheriff and Lynchburg Police Department and solicited their support. Then the pastor's wife and Milton's mother boarded a bus to Lynchburg.

The Amherst Sheriff's Department provided the name and address of the man who had driven Ron to Amherst and who had assumed responsibility for Milton. The Lynchburg Police Department provided an officer and a cruiser to help them locate the baby-sitter. When they were able to contact the man who had Milton, they found that Milton had been placed in the care of yet another stranger.

Arriving at the new address, they found Milton playing in the yard. When his mother stepped from the police car, he ran to her exclaiming, "Mommy, Mommy!"

After taking Milton into their custody, the officer drove the two women and Milton to the bus station in Lynchburg and waited until the bus for New York departed just to be sure there was no problem.

As one might guess, Ron filed a lawsuit against the pastor's wife, in which he claimed she came down from New York and kidnapped Milton aided by the Lynchburg Police Department, Amherst County Sheriffs Department, Amherst County Social Services, and others, including Sheryl and me because, as in all of his lawsuits involving any of his children, he alleged that we were the real criminal kidnappers, the cause of all his problems. He never once mentioned that Milton's mother was merely accompanied by the other lady, a fact he hoped the court wouldn't notice.

Before he left the U. A. E. for America, Ron obtained a warrant there charging me with kidnapping. The last I heard it was on file with Interpol. Ron had also impersonated a journalist and wrote an article that was published in a Persian Gulf newspaper alleging that Oshia and I had been tried in absentia (not present), convicted of kidnapping, and sentenced to life in prison. The newspaper, without making any effort to contact me, printed the article.

I learned of this nonsense when I was called into the office by the Vice-President and Plant Superintendent where I worked one afternoon. They presented me with a "WANTED" poster they had received in the mail. Ron evidently thought it would get me fired, but it didn't work.

The "WANTED" poster had my picture on it, the one which had been taken at Myrtle Beach, South Carolina. The caption read, "Wanted for kidnapping and suspected child molestation." This was followed by a lot of other nonsense including the claim that I had already been tried, convicted, and sentenced to life in prison. It also offered a reward for Shana's return to her mother (from whom he abducted her in the first place). He also claimed that I was, "Armed and extremely dangerous." I had a hunting rifle, a target rifle, and a shotgun. The article said that Shana "Was held under constant armed guard by the members of the church." The poster and its accusations were just one of many cruel attempts to assassinate our character and good name.

As I glanced over the poster, I chuckled then added, "Oh, no, he's up to his old tricks again!" I had come to expect such accusations from him

Following a brief explanation of what was going on, my employers confided that they had called the police first to confirm whether there were any charges pending against me and found none. Their concern was that if he came for me it might jeopardize the safety of my fellow employees, but Ron, up to this point anyway, though very malicious, had not been nervy enough to wield a gun. He would rather get someone else to do his dirty work for him.

I concluded that in addition to trying to get me fired he also hoped to stir up some militant Muslims against me by stating that "this was a religious kidnapping to change this child's religion from Islam to Christianity," which was totally false. I didn't have any idea how many people he had sent those posters to or what some people might believe.

First, I did not kidnap Shana as I later tried to explain to him in court, and second, Shana was already a Christian when he abducted her, not Muslim. He claimed she knew the whole Koran, prayed five times a day in the mosque (though according to Shana woman don't go to the mosques to pray - only the men do), and that she "was actually the 'golden child,' a prodigy of Islam." He also said, "She speaks, reads, and writes Arabic fluently as well as speaking two other languages."

When learning of his claim, Shana responded, "I cannot!"

When the custody issue finally came before the court, the judge reviewed other cases similar to this one and the circumstances surrounding it as the facts were presented. It is normally assumed that when there is a custody dispute between a parent and a non-parent, it is in the best interest of the child to be placed in the custody of the parent, but due to some previous cases the Virginia Supreme Court has established five guidelines by which this assumption can be rebutted in lower courts. This case involved all five of them. Basically the guidelines or factors considered by the court and their relations to this case are as follows:

> *1. Unfitness - "Mr. Simon's unfitness was exhibited in his lifestyle, attitude, behavior, instability, living circumstances, personal habits, and emotional status," according to the court order. Although Ron was a rather intelligent person he did not appear to be gainfully employed, he did not have a regular place of residence, could not keep a permanent wife who could be a motherly figure for Shana, even though he claimed several wives, at least two of which lived with him at the same time. In Virginia bigamy and polygamy are both considered felonies (also contrary to Muslim customs). As a result, housekeeping suffered according to Social Service reports. He was still living in his mother's home, but his mother was living in Maryland at the time.*

> *2. Previous Divestiture - "Mr. 'Simon' was previously divested of custody of 'Shana' by order of the New York Court."*

> *3. Voluntary Relinquishment - "Mr. 'Simon' relinquished custody of the child to Mr. and Mrs. 'Richards' when she was an infant.*

4. Abandonment - "Mr. 'Simon' abandoned the child for two and one-half years." For over two years he had no contact with her by phone or by mail.

5. Special Circumstances - "Mr. 'Simon' has disobeyed court orders in New York and Virginia on three occasions by taking the child out of the jurisdiction of the appropriate court and away from the custodial parties. The child indicated a desire to live with Mr. and Mrs. 'Richards' and not to see Mr. 'Simon.'"

After having considered the circumstances surrounding this case and other similar case histories, the court concluded it was in Shana's best interest, to be placed in our custody with only supervised visitation at Ron's expense.

"I just do not trust him," commented Judge Jacobs.

Ron's court appointed attorney indicated he would file an appeal (at Ron's insistence). Mr. Rodger Grimes from Social Services volunteered to supervise the visits until the case was concluded, but as we shall see the case can never be concluded as far as Ron is concerned, unless it is to his satisfaction.

Both in the Juvenile & Domestic Relations Court and also in the Circuit Court, to which the first decision was appealed, Ron's allegations and accusations against us, plus a couple of character witnesses on our side, consumed so much time that a second hearing had to be scheduled.

During this extended process, Ron received the supervised visitations. Shana confided that Ron was taking her for walks in the back yard at his mother's house. His mother's house was facing one fork of a road and the back yard faced the other fork. We knew it would be a simple matter to park a car on the other fork of the road, and if he could sneak Shana across the backyard to the other fork, he would stuff her in the car and be gone like he did in New York.

We had advised Shana to yell if he tried anything like that, but she felt subjected to him, and we weren't sure if she would. So we alerted Mr. Grimes who was supervising the visits and also wrote a warning letter to our attorney, which she copied and forwarded to the other parties involved. Sure enough, on one of these visits, Ron took her to the basement to play video games. Once in the basement, he tried to sneak her out of the house. When Mr. Grimes heard the door open, he looked out to see them in the back yard. Realizing he had been discovered, Ron returned to the basement leaving the door ajar this time.

After a short while, Ron slipped out with Shana again. Rodger, hearing no sound of activity in the basement, checked the backyard again and, seeing Ron halfway across the backyard in a trot holding onto Shana's hand, gave prompt pursuit. Ron had already put Shana in the back seat and jumped into the driver's seat when Rodger reached the car. Rodger was able to get the passenger door open and get a foot inside as Ron started the car and took off attempting to throw Rodger off the car as he clung to the door.

Somehow Rodger managed to hang on until he could get hold of the steering wheel and pull himself inside where the two men scuffled until they broke the key off in the ignition.

As the car came to a stop, Ron kept repeating, "This is the only way Rodger; it's the only way."

As the car stopped, Ron jumped out and ran. After instructing Shana to run and lock herself in his pickup truck, Rodger gave chase after Ron, but soon returned to his truck since Ron had a head start and may have out run him. As Rodger and Shana drove off, Ron circled around and attempted to overtake them.

"He's going to catch us! I know he is!" Shana was exclaiming as they made their getaway.

A few minutes later, Rodger showed up at Sheryl's place of employment, red faced and puffing from exhaustion, and asked her to call the police for him.

"What happened?" She inquired as she dialed the police number.

"He tried to take off with Shana," Rodger declared.

After reporting the attempted abduction Rodger and Shana returned to the scene where they were met by the police. Apparently Ron thought maybe Rodger was taking Shana back to school after their confrontation and maybe he could intercept them along the way. Whatever he was planning, he had driven off in his car, but returned home a short while later and was promptly taken into custody.

When he was arrested, he had in his pocket airline tickets to Tokyo, Japan, and Shana's passport, which Oshia had snuck out of the house and given to Ron. (When we discovered she had double crossed us by taking the passport and given it to Ron, in violation of the protective custody order she had filed against him, we lost confidence that she could be trusted and, therefore, had to evict her from our home for Shana's safety as well as our own. When she first came to the United States, we did not know how long she would be here and she really had nowhere else to go. We had allowed her to live with us, but no more. After a short stay in a local shelter, she needled her way to California where Jinny had been born. Since then, she has been granted refugee status, has married, has another child, and seems to be doing okay.

Ron was charged with attempted abduction and assault on a state employee, but later the assault charge on Mr. Grimes was dropped in favor of the attempted abduction, a felony charge in Virginia and probably easier to prosecute. Prior to the hearing, Ron was released on his own recognizance and shortly thereafter began conspiring with a man he met in jail whom he thought he could get to abduct Shana for him.

At first Ron offered to sell the man his mother's house at a cheap price and later offered to give it to him if he would do the job for him. Of course, the house was not his to sell or give away, because it belonged to his mother, and Craig still had the power of attorney for her.

Later an agreement was reached between Craig, his mother's bank, and one of their attorneys to sell the house because it was deteriorating, and Dr. Simon was no longer able to live there alone. As was Ron's practice, he either filed suit or threatened to file suit against the parties involved for the illegal sale of his mother's house even though the court approved it.

When the jailhouse acquaintance asked Ron what he should do about Sheryl and me if we got in the way, Ron told him to do whatever he had to do to get his daughter back. I'm not sure if he said to kill us or not, but apparently Ron implied that would be okay with him if necessary. As a result, the individual, not wanting to get into any more trouble, notified the police. He granted the police permission to record his phone conversations with Ron, but could not get enough incriminating evidence to support a conspiracy to commit a felony charge.

As the scheduled hearing date approached, the court received a letter from Ron stating that he would not be able to keep the appointment since he was scheduled to appear in a California case involving his other daughter Jinny about the same time. Whether it was the scheduling or what, his appearance here in Virginia had priority. However, since the authorities here had no further contact with him as the date approached they decided to postpone the hearing, release witnesses, and proceed to charge him with contempt of court when he did not appear.

A warrant was issued for his arrest, and when the F. B. I. was investigating a bad check Ron wrote for the unconfirmed amount of $37,000, they discovered that Ron was wanted in Virginia and locked him up pending extradition. This time the Lynchburg Commonwealth Attorney's Office was obliged to act. A new hearing was scheduled and, as a result, Ron was convicted of attempted abduction and served about eighteen months of a five-year sentence. It was during this hearing that I happened to meet my would-be assassin and assured him that he had done the right thing by notifying police. Later we sat together and conversed during another hearing.

This really blew Ron's mind. In all cases involving a jury, Ron tried to be sure there would be no Christians, friends, or members of local Baptist churches approved. This was especially true in the attempted abduction case, but he must have missed some who later told us they were on the jury that convicted him. I was excluded as an observer on the premises that I might be called as a witness so I had to rely on Sheryl and the newspaper for an account of the events. During the hearing, Ron pressed his court appointed attorney to tout his accomplishments, his travels, his books, and his I.Q.

During his summary, the judge told Ron, "Mr. Simon, you may have an I.Q. of 200, which may be equal to the combined total of everyone in this courtroom; you have written four books which probably are four more than anyone here has written; you have traveled the world over and done many other things most of us have never done but there is something radically wrong with you."

In another hearing Ron, representing himself, kept insisting that I had kidnapped Shana.

I finally responded, "Ron, you have a mind set that I kidnapped Shana, yet I did no such thing. You're a smart man. You know the meaning of the word 'kidnapping.' It means 'to take someone by force or against their will' and I did neither."

"Well, how did they [Shana and Oshia] get over here?"

"They said they wanted to come and I provided them with airline tickets." I replied.

"How do you know they wanted to come?" He quipped.

"Well, I've got a phone and they can talk. Is that too hard for you to understand?"

Whether it was included with this case or separately, Ron was also convicted on the contempt of court charge as well, but he appealed this charge to no avail, claiming that he could not be in contempt of court because the hearing had been postponed. However, the hearing was postponed because it was determined he would not show up. That's the confusion game Ron seems to enjoy playing, but the judges are not as stupid as he portrays them to be and they have the edge in authority.

A young friend of mine, who is known as "Tiny," complete with the irony of standing 6 feet tall and weighing well over 200 pounds, was employed by the Lynchburg Police Department. I later bumped into him at a birthday party, and found out Tiny was selected to accompany the investigator when extraditing Ron from California. On the return flight, Ron was handcuffed to the investigator, who had to accompany him to the bathroom. While they were gone, Tiny picked up a book Ron had left in his seat and began to read it. It was one of several Ron had written, this on the subject of Thomas Jefferson's slave children. In the preface, Ron clearly libeled us by claiming that we had kidnapped Shana while he and his family were living in the U. A. E. It included our names and address.

When Ron returned to his seat, Tiny said to him, "Ron, I know these people and I don't believe a word of this."

In response Ron launched into one of his tirades about our evils.

This young police officer friend of ours said he was fed up and warned Ron saying, "I've heard enough of this nonsense, so shut up before I throw you off of this plane!"

Ron immediately turned to the investigator and said, "Did you hear him threaten me?"

"Frankly it crossed my mind, too," was his only response.

I recently mentioned this to Craig, who chuckled and said, "If they had thrown him off the plane maybe we all could have lived more peaceful lives."

Several people have suggested I file a libel suit against him, but my response has been, "Why?" You can't get blood out of a turnip. Why spend more money and get nothing in return? Ron has nothing and he won't work. Furthermore, if anyone took this case it would have to be on a contingency basis. It would involve international libel laws since it was published in Berkley, California, and printed in Tokyo, Japan, and even if one could win the case I doubt if the proceeds from all the books Ron has sold would offset the cost.

This attempted abduction took place during a supervised visitation. It was during the interval between scheduled hearings in the circuit court on his appeal of the custody decision. When the hearings in Amherst County resumed, the testimony of Rodger Grimes and the investigating officer from Lynchburg were also brought into this case.

After hearing their testimony Judge Goode said to Ron, "I can't believe you did this. I would have given you unlimited visitation."

During the Circuit Court hearing, Craig flew up from South Carolina to testify for us on Shana's behalf as he had done in the J & D Court. Also, the J & D Court ordered psychological evaluations. The psychiatrist, considered expert testimony as to what was best for the child, also recommended Shana remain in our custody based on the evaluations.

At the conclusion, the judge upheld the J & D Court's ruling and informed Ron that, "I will not discuss visitation until you prove to this court that you can be trusted. Frankly, I don't know how you're going to do it, but that's up to you. My door is open." That was the fall of 1991, and Ron never made an effort to do so.

In the midst of these legal battles Sheryl and I, along with over sixty-five other defendants from all over the world, were charged in a 100 million dollar combined lawsuit of conspiring to kidnap Ron's children and to steal his mother's money. Most of the defendants had never heard of each other let alone been involved together in a worldwide conspiracy of which Sheryl and I were accused of being the instigators.

When one informant relayed this claim to us, Sheryl exclaimed, "Gee, I didn't know we were that powerful!"

This list of defendants included essentially everyone who had in anyway obstructed the exercise of his absolute sovereignty over those for whom he claimed responsibility, including his children and his mother. Ron has not yet learned that only Jehovah God is sovereign. While the Scriptures do not use that descriptive term, it is implied throughout. (See Ephesians 1:11; Psalms 103:19; Proverbs 16:9,33; Lamentations 3:37; and Daniel 5:20,21.)

Included on Ron's list were Sheryl and I, our attorney; Craig and his attorney; Ron's uncle and his attorney; the bank that held his mother's trust account and their attorneys; the judge that froze his mother's trust account and all other attorneys that represented any of his opponents; any judges that ruled against him; and law enforcement agencies or their personnel that constrained him in any way, whether in or out of jail; the airlines that flew his mother and daughter back to the USA; and relatives of Rafiah. Also included were agencies that did not give Ron the support he thought he deserved, such as the US State Department, their various embassies and their personnel, as well as the principal of Temple Christian School and the Pastor and Assistant Pastors of Temple Baptist Church. There were 65-70 defendants in all.

In order to recover damages, one must prove the allegations against the entity thereby charged and furnish a fairly accurate account of the loss or damage thus sustained by each. Reading the first page of these claims, it was easy to see why the first such lawsuit never made it on the court docket. When the district judge met with some of the lawyers who would be representing their clients, he declined to hear the case and dismissed it without going to court.

Refusing to accept defeat, Ron filed the same lawsuit a short time later in a federal court in New York, where it was also dismissed after routine filing of demurs. At first we were a little concerned, but concluded that we were little fish in the big pond and if the larger ones were able to defend themselves, we would be overlooked and it was so.

Concerned that our defense against Ron's frivolous lawsuits was costing us a lot of money unnecessarily, our attorney filed a $300,000.00 counter-suit against him to break it up. In Virginia, when such a case is filed, the defendant must respond within twenty-one days or lose by default no matter how frivolous the charge. Whether Ron stayed on the move so much that he wasn't aware of the counter-suit or whether he chose to ignore it is not clear, but the deadline passed without any response. The next step in the procedure was to get a court date set for a hearing to determine what damages were applicable. We did not keep a day-to-day tabulation of expenses, but estimated our legal expenses before, during, and after the second abduction, including those in Thailand and the plane tickets for Shana and Oshia's return, to be in the neighborhood of $40,000.00.

When our attorney asked me how this had affected us, without thinking, I replied, "It aggravated me more than anything."

I think it was one of Ron's goals to drive us into bankruptcy. (He later found out that we had mortgaged our house to pay off legal fees so he conspired with someone to try to buy up our mortgage and have us evicted, but failed.) During the hearing, in which he represented himself, he questioned us about whether Craig had loaned us any money.

"No," I replied.

"Did your church give you any money?"

"No."

"Did Thomas Road Baptist Church give you any money?"

"No."

"Where did you get it then?"

"We both work," I replied.

We had actually accumulated a little bit here and there - insurance settlement, sold some property to the state when they needed to widen the road in front of our house, and Sheryl's sister left her a little at the time of her death. At the conclusion of the hearing, the judge's ruling awarded us a total judgment of $31,000.

He told our attorney he would have made it a little more if it were not for the remark I made when I said that it aggravated me more than anything. I guess I was supposed to say, "It nearly ruined us financially," which was close to being true, but I didn't want Ron to know. We were badly bent - but not broken.

"Well, when I see the first penny, then I will regret that I didn't say the right thing." I told our attorney. From that day to this I haven't seen the first penny and never expect to.

Later another hearing was scheduled, during which I was granted what I really wanted - an injunction forbidding Ron, or anyone acting on his behalf, from filing any more lawsuits or other legal documents against us in Virginia courts based on allegations, theories, or issues previously brought before the Lynchburg Circuit Court. This included all issues regarding any of Ron's children. If he fails to comply with any of the terms of the injunction, he will be found in contempt of court and punished accordingly.

Since he was running out of options, Ron decided that maybe he could get the case heard before a different judge who wasn't fully aware of his behavior pattern. He filed a petition for custody and/or visitation in the Lynchburg, Virginia, J & D Court. This being a district court, the same judge may preside over cases in another court in the same district when the regular judge is on vacation, sick, or otherwise unavailable. On the date of the scheduled hearing, when we were assembled in the court room and the judge entered, it was the same judge who had originally heard the case in the Amherst J & D Court and had ruled against Ron. This amused us, but it flabbergasted Ron when Judge Jacobs began informing him that he was in the wrong court because the Amherst courts retained jurisdiction of his case instead of Lynchburg.

As Ron stood to object and begin telling Judge Jacobs what he could and could not do, the judge interrupted him saying, "You have a court appointed attorney - maybe he can explain it to you."

Eventually Ron re-filed the same petition in Amherst J & D Court. The injunction was not to be construed as denying him access to J & D or Family Court in pursuing custody or visitation of any of his children in the event of the emergence of new issues or facts regarding the same. The only new issues or facts he could cite were (1) Shana was older, and (2) she was taller.

She did not want to live with him or visit with him since he had tried to abduct her a third time. She let her wishes be made known by writing a note to her Guardian Ad Litem. Since Ron still had plans to take her from the area if granted custody, plus the fact that she did not want to go, the petition was denied prompting an automatic appeal by Ron.

Back in the Circuit Court, a retired justice of the Virginia Supreme Court was selected to hear the case since local judges wanted nothing to do with Ron. This time Shana was a little less shy and clearly testified that she did not want to live with him or even visit with him. She chose to remain in contact with him by mail. This judge, like the others, denied Ron's appeal, but added, "When you submit to this court a plan for supervised visitation that this court can approve, only then can we discuss visitation."

As was his custom, Ron expressed his displeasure by writing critical, insulting letters to the judge in which he claimed that the judge ordered Shana's Guardian Ad Litem to submit the plan for visitation and then reneged when he failed to do so. This was absolutely untrue. From the Circuit Court, it was appealed to the Virginia Court of Appeals and the Virginia Supreme Court then the United States Supreme Court being denied at each step, as it was the first time through. The only difference was that we both represented ourselves. Our attorney had given up her private practice following our first major victory in the Circuit Court when Ron was convicted of attempted abduction.

One interesting lesson I learned from a justice of the U.S. Supreme Court was that we could not lose by default like in the Virginia courts without having had ample opportunity to respond. If, after reviewing the case records from the lower courts, they decided to hear the case, then and only then would we be required to respond by notification and given thirty days to do so. The major difference here though, was that we would have to provide forty copies of our brief. Understandably we did not want to go to this trouble if unnecessary.

Sheryl had become quite adept at editing other court pleadings to fit our particular situation and her skill proved quite valuable in some of our latest responses. Sometime in late 1994 or early 1995 we were subpoenaed to appear at a civil suit hearing in Lynchburg Circuit Court in which Ron was charging that a Lynchburg police officer and the Amherst County Sheriff had helped kidnap his son Milton. At that hearing he produced a paper that he said gave him custody of Shana so he had to make copies available to all. It was a handwritten court order supposedly modifying the June 7, 1992 New York Supreme Court order which divested him of custody of Shana in favor of Rafiah, but now granting him custody by default of the mother.

The first thing that aroused my suspicion was that it was hand-written. In this computer age one would think a court order would at least be printed, especially by the New York State Supreme Court. As we returned home and began to study this document, my blood began to boil. I remember hearing someone say that Ron had been informed that there was nothing the court could do for him unless he had a court order giving him custody of Shana so obviously, this was his plan to get one.

On October 7, 1994, he revisited the court where the original custody decision had been made. It was the same court that declined to reverse the order about a year after he had abducted Shana when she was nine months old. By this time the justice who made the original decision had either retired or died. The justice that modified the original order either had not been on the Supreme Court in 1992 or knew little or nothing about the case. She apparently didn't bother to find out anything, but fell for everything Ron told her, which was that on or about October 1, 1982, the mother had abandoned him and Shana to return to her native Pakistan and had not returned to the U.S.

What he didn't tell this justice, I'm sure, is that he had abducted the child in violation of the New York court order about a month and a half after it was handed down and a little over two months before Rafiah left the U.S. Also, here was a twenty-year-old girl, who according to her testimony, had been abused on her honeymoon, in a strange country, unable to speak the language except through an interpreter, desiring to return to the familiarity of her homeland and her family.

By the rules of Islam, which governed her country, the women

97

were underprivileged. Their main responsibility was to bear children and serve their husbands. That doesn't sound too bad in itself, but women were not considered worth educating in many circumstances or maybe they couldn't afford an education due to the poor economy. Rafiah came from a very remote village in the Himalayan Mountains where they lived in mud huts, and the birth mortality rate was around 50 percent according to Ron. In her religion, the fathers owned the children and the mothers had no custody rights. Even though she was granted custody in the U.S., she did not have the means or the ambition to wage a battle against Ron, whom she was probably afraid of and logically wanted to get away from and forget about at this point.

In addition, if Rafiah returned to her country with a baby and no husband it would look bad on her. Then too, her country did not have a welfare program to assist her, and it would make it more difficult for a separated wife with a baby to find a good husband.

Missionaries, who understand this particular culture, say that mothers do not get too attached to their daughters because they will be married off at a young age. Maybe this is one reason Ron was so determined to retain/regain custody of Shana - to collect a sizable dowry for her or perhaps he had already made a commitment to some of his Muslim friends and could not deliver. This is not to say that all of their customs are wrong. In fact, they are similar to old Jewish customs, but they are certainly different to what most of us are used to, however, and we need to understand what Rafiah had been taught in order to understand her actions, why she was willing to leave without her daughter in order to get away from Ron.

The point is that Shana's mother did not abandon Ron and the child as he claimed because he had already abducted Shana from her mother's custody a little over two months before. He claimed he was afraid she would try to take the child back to Pakistan with her. Actually, I believe he did the right thing, but for the wrong reason. On top of the other lies, he told the judge that he had been the de-facto custodial parent since the mother's departure and that he had provided the child with a caring and stable home environment for twelve years ('82-'94).

When I read the claims Ron had made, I wrote a letter to the clerk of the New York Supreme Court, which Sheryl typed and mailed.

It read: "This looks like some kind of joke to me, but if there is any validity to it whatsoever please be informed that Mr. Simon has presented this court with false information."

Enclosed with the letter was the modified court order, the certified court orders from the Amherst County J & D and Circuit Courts, proving that the events of the past twelve years were anything but as described by Ron, except perhaps the time Shana spent with us. Of course that was even complicated during the last four years by his onslaught of lawsuits.

A few days or perhaps a week or two had passed when Sheryl received a phone call from the clerk of the New York Supreme Court. He apologized because, as he said, they didn't know about these proceedings. He said he understood how we felt, but relief would have to be sought through proper legal proccdurcs, which mcant we would have to file a petition to vacate the modified order.

The New York judge agreed that Amherst County Courts should have the jurisdiction to settle this dispute and that he would confirm that by a court order or other correspondence if necessary. This technicality was overlooked when Ron fled with Shana in 1986 and was apparently forgotten afterwards. We figured this was why he kept insisting there was no court order transferring jurisdiction to Virginia. A show cause order was sent out which allowed Ron to argue his claims some more and he took advantage of it. Since the very beginning when he felt things weren't going his way, he resorted to character assassination, accusing us of kidnapping and traumatizing Shana, outright lies, allegations, half truths, distortion of facts, saying one or the other of us was stupid, fat, lazy, in poor health, etc.

As was previously noted, his false statements and half-truths were too numerous to respond to, but we drafted a response to a few of them. One in particular I could not let go unchecked. He claimed we were the ones who wanted the jurisdiction transferred to Virginia. Neither he nor Rafiah had ever agreed that Virginia had jurisdiction over this case. I requested copies of our custody petitions from the J & D Court clerk proving that his petition was filed prior to ours and I included them with our response.

I added, "I don't know much about law, but I understand that when a person files such a petition in a court they automatically subject themselves to the jurisdiction of that court."

As far as Rafiah was concerned, the only thing that appeared to bother her was the possibility that Ron might regain custody of Shana. Ron has frequently complained that Shana should have been returned to the custody of her parents, but how can that be accomplished when they are thousands of miles apart. Not to mention the fact that he is the one who abducted Shana from Rafiah in the first place? After reviewing the responses and "more complete evidence and information in the matter" the modified order was vacated and Ron was advised to "pursue his remedies in Virginia."

Chapter 13

Close Encounters

On several occasions after picking up Shana from school, Sheryl spotted Ron tailing her in traffic as she was headed home. This caused her concern as Ron was under court order to have no physical contact, to stay on the Lynchburg side of the James River, and not to enter Madison Heights at all. The school and our home were both in Madison Heights. He had already proven that he could not be trusted. Knowing he had also tried to hire a hit man, you can imagine how unnerving it was for Sheryl to find Ron in the rear view mirror.

Sheryl suspected that Ron was hiding behind a building across the street from the school. She propositioned our youngest son, Jake, to take off early from work one afternoon and to park in an area that would give him a good vantage point to be on the lookout. On the appointed day, Jake and his wife, Dawn, parked in the lot in front of the empty building. His position was facing the bank, with the empty building slightly behind him to his right and the school driveway clearly visible to his left side. All was clear - there were no signs of Ron or a vehicle. Jake's initial thought was that his stakeout was in vain, but just as he saw Sheryl's car coming up the driveway from the school, a tall, lanky figure appeared from behind the bank and started up the hill towards the lot where Jake and Dawn were parked.

Jake had met Ron before, but it had been years. Though Jake did not recognize Ron he was naturally suspicious of the man because he was sitting there in the first place. He watched as the figure disappeared behind the empty building.

"He's got a car parked behind there!" Jake exclaimed.

As Sheryl pulled out onto the highway, Jake quickly started his own car, put it in reverse, and stomped on the gas. He was just in time to cut Ron off and block his route.

Ron was rattled and got out of his car from the passenger side yelling, "Who are you? Who are you?"

As Ron approached their car, Jake sped forward. In his haste, Ron had failed to put his car in park or put the parking break on and his car began rolling down the lot toward the highway, which was busy with traffic. He was able to run and jump in and stop the vehicle just before it reached the highway. Once again, he got out and was shouting at Jake, who was now out of his own vehicle and ready with his camera. The picture, later used in court against him, clearly showed Ron at Highway 29 in Madison Heights. The sign and business behind him, located next to the school, proved that he had violated yet another court order.

It was only a few weeks later when Jake had another close encounter with Ron. This time it was at the local public school during an election. Jake recognized Ron this time, but pretended not to know him. One would think that given the previous encounter being so recent that Ron would have recognized Jake also, but apparently he did not. He approached Jake and handed him a piece of paper. That's normal at voting poles, but what was out of place was Ron. He still was not supposed to be in Madison Heights. Jake examined the paper and what he read made his blood boil. It was an 8 ½" x 11" sheet containing lies about both Sheryl and me. We were accused of kidnapping and keeping Shana captive. Ron gave our full names, social security numbers, phone number, and address. How wicked! The man had no shame propagating his lies in the community where we lived. No doubt those who knew us would know better than to believe what was in print, but the very principle of it was infuriating.

On his way back to his car Jake had to pass by Ron again and it required a great deal of self-restraint. Jake was trembling with anger. What he really wanted to do was drag Ron off behind some cars and cause him some gross discomfort. He managed to only speak instead.

"Hello Ron." He said in a very cool tone and as civil as he could offer under the circumstances.

Ron was more than curious. "How do you know my name?" He asked nervously.

Jake made no reply but kept walking.

Ron persisted trailing Jake and repeating the question several times; "How do you know my name? How do you know my name? How do you know my name?"

They were getting closer to the cars, and Jake realized that his innermost desire could become a reality. It certainly seemed feasible and even appealed to him as a viable option, yet we had told him in the past that if we continued to give Ron enough rope he'd eventually hang himself. Jake also knew that the scripture says, "Vengeance is mine. I will repay saith the Lord" (Deuteronomy 32:34).

"You don't want to know." Was Jake's only reply before getting in his car and driving off, thanking God for the power to resist temptation.

Chapter 14

A Satanic Death-wish Unfulfilled

As was previously mentioned, Ron was involved in the writing of several books, one of which detailed how to orchestrate the hostile takeover of a struggling American public company by bidding slightly higher than the stock's appraised value thereby forcing a sale to the highest bidder. Thus Ron is believed to have been involved in assisting a Japanese publisher friend of his in the acquisition of a printing company in California.

Eventually we received a copy of a book published by this Japanese publisher, which was portrayed as an addition to the Holy Bible, but was mostly about Numerology, a satanic religion common in the Far East. Inside we found some derogatory insults pertaining to Sheryl's given name. Ron claims he did not write the book, but it was obvious this was his input because this publisher did not know us nor did we know him. This religion portrayed Yahweh as a vicious, mean spirited, war-mongering god, while a sketch of a scantily clad woman represented a 'loving goddess.' Also included was a death wish. "Die ye followers of Yahweh" (God of Israel).

This upset Craig somewhat. I assured him that if he were a child of God (which he claimed to be) that Satan couldn't harm him (Psalms 34:7).

With this assurance, we proceeded to Hilton Head Island, South Carolina, to enjoy our vacation with Shana. Being a real estate secretary, Sheryl was interested in availability, development, and prices in resort communities. A couple we had met who lived in Hilton Head Plantation, a restricted subdivision, got us a pass and we went exploring. After a short while, a dark cloud formed and it began to rain. We had intended to locate the area where this couple lived, but because of the storm, visibility was very poor and there appeared to be no place to park except in someone's driveway. We decided to head back to the main road and toward our timeshare unit. When we reached the main road and turned in that direction, I elected to turn into the first parking lot I saw to wait out the storm.

We found a strip mall of flat roofed buildings joined together. We made ourselves comfortable and prepared to wait for the rain to stop or at least slacken. After a little while it did let up a little so Sheryl got the bright idea to go shopping to take advantage of the lull.

"Come on," she said to Shana. "Let's not waste our time sitting here in the car. Let's see what these stores have for sale."

There was a Polly Flinders on the right end, a Pfaltzgraff store on to the left of that and other stores on down the line. Sheryl's first intention was to visit the Pfaltzgraff store to look at some dishes, but changed her mind and decided to visit the end store first.

"I might find some clothes for my granddaughter," she told Shana.

They hadn't been in the store but a little while when Sheryl said she heard a rumbling sound and water began leaking into the corner of the store.

"What's going on?" She asked the cashier.

"I don't know but we'd better get out of here." She advised.

They hadn't much more than gotten to the sidewalk when the roof of the Pfaltzgraff store collapsed under the weight of the water. Apparently, it couldn't drain fast enough due to the flat roof. Right in the corner where the dishes were, right where Sheryl and Shana would have been if she had followed her first inclination, the roof caved in! Since I'm not much of a shopper I had remained in the car and was shocked when they told me what had happened.

Then I remembered the death-wish/threat. Not only did I thank the Lord for deliverance (Psalms 34:7), but chuckled and said, "Well Satan, you old devil, you missed us this time."

I'm sure glad no one else was hurt if he was aiming for us. What caused Sheryl to change her mind and go into the Polly Flinders store first? Read the following scriptures for the answer. (Psalms 37:23; Proverbs 3:5,6; 16:9, 33; 20:24; Isaiah 55:8,9; and Jeremiah 10:23)

Conclusion

Your My Parents seems at times like a nightmare when I think back and relive some of the events, but the events actually happened. It is true and even though this chapter is titled "Conclusion" it still has an open door at the end - things can still happen and probably will, but it is doubtful they will be any more significant than those that have already transpired. The one crowning event if it should happen - and we keep praying that it will - is for Ron to be saved, to receive Jesus Christ as his Lord and Savior. Then and only then will he be able to understand why we took the action that we did. Then and only then will there be any basis for a meaningful relationship between him and Shana. I would not wish eternity in Hell on my worst enemy, but it is sure for those who reject/neglect God's salvation (John 3:16; Hebrews 2:3). Though Ron once faked a conversion at a local church, to obtain our favor and to attend a church play that Shana participated in, his later actions did not reflect a changed heart. There was no evidence of a true relationship with God.

Incidentally, after Shana returned to the U. S. A. she was tested and allowed to enter the fourth grade. Although she had little if any formal education after kindergarten, tests determined her to be as knowledgeable as the average person her age. With a little help from a young teacher, she caught up that year, made about half A's in the fifth grade and practically all A's in the sixth and seventh grades before transferring to Lynchburg Christian Academy (L. C. A.), so she only attended nine grades out of twelve. (Sharp kid, I'd say.)

We hope that we will be a respected influence in Shana's life for years to come, but most of all that she will heed the words of Proverbs 3:5,6; "Trust in the Lord with all thine heart; and lean not unto thine own understanding. In all thy ways acknowledge Him, and He shall direct thy paths."

107

As was stated previously, we were not in search of another child to raise when we got involved with Shana, since we had already become grandparents. (I was 48 years of age and Sheryl was 43.) Our desire to gain custody of Shana grew out of the fact that Ron was not a good role model for her, and it was clear that if she were going to have a decent chance in life, we were going to have to be channels of God's grace in providing it for her. This was no problem because she was so loving and lovable. We went through many valleys in the process, but the Lord was with us. When He brought us through victoriously it was worth the effort. I cannot and do not gloat over Ron's defeat in the courts, but rather give God the honor and glory and praise because He gave us the victory for Shana's sake. His word tells us in I John 5:14; "And this is the confidence that we have in him, that, if we ask anything according to his will, he heareth us," and we knew without a doubt He would "have all men [and women] to be saved, and to come unto the knowledge of the truth" (I Timothy 2:4, II Peter 3:9).

Of course, we cannot emphasize God's Word in court because Ron tries to portray us as religious fanatics or members of a cult. On one such occasion I responded to his attorney's questioning by saying, "We are not religious fanatics. In fact, we don't believe in religion at all and while we don't believe the court is the place to settle religious issues, we do believe the Bible and we are born again believers according to God's Word. We believe God said what He meant and meant what He said and we take Him seriously. If this is your definition of a religious fanatic then so be it."

Ron has tried continuously and failed to assassinate our character. Those who know us know better and those who don't know us probably don't care. Ron's vicious attacks against us and others, with whom he doesn't agree, have been spread all over the Internet. Were it not for the necessity of protecting the identity of those involved we would have loved to share some of his nonsense along with news articles and court orders because they would definitely create more enthusiasm for reading *You're My Parents*. If any of you readers who are also computer Web surfers accidentally stumble onto Ron's articles, just remember: you can't believe anything you hear and only half of what you see. It is, after all, just his point of view. The fact that every court decision has been in our favor proves that others saw things differently than Ron and that strengthened our faith in God (Proverbs 3:5,6; Proverbs 16:2,9,23; Proverbs 21:1; Jeremiah 10:23; Lamentations 3:37; Daniel 4:32,33).

I'll be the first to admit that I am not worthy of God's blessings (Romans 5:8; I Timothy 1:15), however, I will not question God's sovereignty for His choices are not based on our worthiness, but on our willingness to do His will. I've often wondered why He chose us for this task, and I've concluded it must be because of our stubbornness and determination to stand firm in the face of adversity, an essential quality for those who would serve in God's army – serving God is not for wimps (Luke 9:62; Ephesians 4:14; James 1:8).

I received an interesting phone call one day from a young lady who was a law student at the University of Wisconsin. She had discovered the ridiculous accusations against us, that Ron had posted on his websites and decided this story might be a good subject for her thesis. After contacting Ron and listening to his acidic allegations against us she decided to get our side of the story.

I gave her a few basic facts then I told her; "If you'll promise to send me a copy of your thesis when completed, I'll send you a copy of the court order - that way you'll get it straight from the horse's mouth instead of my opinions, to which she agreed.

In her thesis she stated that after talking to both of us, she was inclined to believe my side of the story, but one thing was certain: "No lawyer in their right mind should want to get involved in a case like that!"

For all practical purposes we considered our story finished when we won the previous court battles, but as we shall see, Ron refused to give up.

Epilogue

In a previous chapter I promised to share more information about a Muslim activist who contacted me from San Pablo, California. I received a telephone call one day from a gentleman with a fairly heavy accent who asked, "Where does this fellow, Ron Simon, get the money to travel all over the world?"

Of course, I didn't have all the information to answer his question accurately; plus I wondered who this guy was and why he wanted to know. I believed however, that it would be fairly accurate to say that most of Ron's money came from his mother with or without her consent. Shana had witnessed his forgeries on his mother's checks while they were living abroad. She told me that she heard arguments between Ron and his mother where he wanted her to sign a check and she wouldn't. He would then sign her name to it anyway.

Before I could answer, he asked, "What kind of man is he?"

I determined by this that he really wanted to know so I opened the bag and let the cat out. I related to him a few basic facts about our story.

As we continued a little farther he said, "They ought to take him out to the middle of the ocean and dump him!!"

By "they," I presumed he meant the militant Muslims who Ron obviously hoped to get stirred up enough to come after me. He had stated on the wanted poster that he sent to my work place accusing me of kidnapping his daughter, that it was a religious kidnapping, to change her religion from Islam to Christianity. Actually, it was just the opposite on two counts. First, Shana had not been taught Islam before coming to us as an infant and when she was old enough to understand, she professed Jesus as her Savior embracing Christianity during the time Ron left her with us. Second, it was Ron who had kidnapped her twice and attempted it a third time.

As it turned out, this Muslim activist was from Pakistan and acquainted with Rafiah's family and the facts surrounding Ron's activities there, so he became more of an ally than an enemy to me. It seems that Ron had persuaded this man to accompany him to a newspaper publisher operated by Indians in San Francisco, California, for an interview. In a previous chapter I mentioned that Ron said he liked the Muslim customs because they were allowed to have up to four wives. How Ron was portrayed didn't seem to bother him too much as long as he got the publicity he craved. During the interview he was bragging about his many wives and children, which at that time was seven children by four different women.

The gentleman told me he asked Ron, "Are you supporting all of these wives and children?"

Ron replied, "Don't need to, they're doing all right on their own."

Actually he's not supporting any of them. The last wife may be supporting him. His initial plan was to put them all on welfare and let the government support them and him - at taxpayer's expense. That's why all the children have U. S. Birth Certificates. When he answered the question about supporting his wives and children the way he did, the Muslim activist got so angry he turned red in the face, according to the reporter. That was why he called me.

I explained to the gentleman that my wife and I did not set out to seek custody of Ron's daughter, although we offered to adopt her if he were willing. As the situation unfolded it seemed that seeking custody was the best solution, and the gentleman agreed, as had the court.

"Just think where she might have ended up if you hadn't been there for her," he said.

As the date of Shana's graduation from high school drew near, she asked me if it would be all right to send Ron an announcement. A week or two before the graduation I received a phone call from a lady in New York wanting to know if it was okay for Ron to come.

"Sure," I told her. "I don't have a problem with that as long as he behaves himself. I think he ought to be able to see his daughter graduate, but tell him not to stir up trouble. If he does, we'll meet it head on!"

Sure enough he showed up driving a yellow New York taxicab. The graduation ceremonies were held in the auditorium of Thomas Road Baptist Church and Ron was seated at one side - almost in a corner where he thought he wouldn't be noticed, I suppose. When he realized he had been discovered and was being watched, he moved to the balcony. Our son Landen followed Ron to the balcony where he could keep an eye on Ron without his being aware that he was still being watched. Everything went smoothly, and after the graduation Shana, accompanied by a couple of her friends, met Ron in the parking lot for a little chat. Her friends were probably curious to see what the kidnapper looked like.

Later Ron posted some pictures on the Internet and complained bitterly that Jerry Falwell (Pastor of Thomas Road Baptist Church and Chancellor of Lynchburg Christian Academy) had shaken his daughter's hand when he handed her diploma to her. Ron stated that neither he nor her mother had given Pastor Falwell permission to do so.

God has warned men not to think of themselves more highly than they ought to think (Romans 12:3, Proverbs 26:12). Ron was quoted by one of his acquaintances as saying that he was the only man alive who had never made a mistake.

After Shana graduated from Lynchburg Christian Academy with honors in 1999, she enrolled in Liberty University where she had a four-year scholarship. After only one year of college she joined the Marines. She had been somewhat of a tomboy most of her life. She was determined not to be outdone by her male friends and she had to prove she was as tough as they were, at least almost as tough. Of course we preferred that she pursue her education first. I think she sensed that we might be reluctant to sign for her to join the military, but when she became eighteen years old, she decided to exercise her independence. We were concerned about the timing of her decision, but supported her anyway. She proved she could take it, and we were privileged to witness her graduation from the Marine Corps boot camp at Paris Island, South Carolina. Graduating from basic training, however, became quite interesting.

Since she was only granted one letter of invitation to orientation and pre-graduation ceremonies, she naturally sent that to us. We had visited her a couple of times during her training, but this time we went down the day before the official graduation drills and ceremonies. We were able to visit with her for several hours during her free time while she tended to some last minute business and then have lunch with her before taking her back to her barracks.

We discovered Ron wandering around outside the food-court and the Marine Museum. She started once to go out and speak to him, but then changed her mind and came back into the food court. When he came in one door looking for her, she went out the other. He walked between Sheryl and I as we stood in line, but never recognized us. Not to be out done, he somehow managed to find out where Shana's barracks were and waited for her to return. We did not go inside when we dropped Shana off, but we would have if we had known he was there. Ron spent some time with Shana in her room. When Ron discovered Shana had been with us most of the evening, he proceeded to contact the local police and the F. B. I. and charge us with kidnapping.

After he left, Shana turned in for the night since she had a long day ahead of her the next day. Some time after she had gone to sleep, she was awakened by the police and F. B. I. agents who questioned her for nearly two hours.

The next morning Sheryl and I went out for breakfast then returned to the motel to freshen up and check out. When we went in, the phone was ringing - it was one of the female officers from the women's division of the U.S. Marine Corps.

"Is this Mrs. Sheryl Richards?" She asked.

"Yes it is," Sheryl replied.

"Shana has something important to tell you so I'm going to let her tell you herself."

"Mom, he's trying to have you and dad arrested again," she said in a worried tone of voice. "He was waiting for me when I returned to my barracks yesterday. He called the police and the F. B. I. and they came and quizzed me for almost two hours."

"Honey, he can't do anything to us so don't let that distract you from what you need to do. We'll be okay," Sheryl assured her.

Then the lady officer took the phone again. "I understand you've been dealing with this for quite awhile."

"Yes, about ten years now," Sheryl replied and gave her a brief synopsis of our involvement with Ron.

"We have the Military Police on alert and we're going to try to keep him off the base," she said, and then added, "I'd like to meet you folks after the ceremonies."

Sure enough, when we reached the base entrance, there was a yellow New York taxicab parked there. Ron was standing by the guardhouse looking down as though he were trimming or cleaning his fingernails and never looked up as we drove by with the invitation letter displayed in the window. Sheryl had bought a new car since he had seen her and he probably wouldn't have recognized her even if he had been looking.

After the ceremonies we had a cordial meeting with the officer Sheryl had spoken with. She also wanted one of us to accompany Shana to the general's office so they could be sure she would be leaving with the right people.

As she was leaving she met one of her comrades and quipped, "I've got one-up on you. I got to meet and shake hands with the brass. If you want to have contacts, you've got to have a screw loose in your family."

As far as I know, Ron never got to see his own daughter graduate from the Marine Corps boot camp because he tried to stir up trouble.

A couple of days after we returned home, I received a phone call from an F. B. I. agent in Beaufort, South Carolina, requesting a little more information about Ron.

"I'm going to put something in the computer system so that if his name turns up again we'll know what kind of man we're dealing with."

"As much trouble as he's caused the F. B. I. and local authorities here in Virginia, I would have thought there would have been something in there about Ron already," I told him.

"Well there's not but I'm going to see that there is from now on."

On several occasions during the foregone custody battles, we were asked if we would allow or encourage Shana to communicate with her mother and explore her culture.

"By all means," we assured them [lawyers and judges]. "In fact, we'll encourage it."

114

We wanted her mother to be aware of her progress because she had expressed her approval and pleasure of our having custody of Shana. Rafiah certainly did not want Ron to gain custody of her. We suggested several times to Shana that her mother would love to hear from her, and I think one time she did write her a few lines, but for the most part she didn't seem to be too interested. It was probably because Ron had drilled it into her head that her mother had abandoned her and didn't care anything about her. This definitely was not the case. It was Ron that Rafiah didn't care too much for.

Eventually Sheryl wrote Rafiah a nice letter and sent her some pictures and other mementos. In time we received a phone call from a lady who lived in New York, but was from Pakistan and was a good friend of Shana's mother. She told us that Rafiah sobbed as she looked at the pictures and said, "I thought I'd never see my daughter again." Rafiah hadn't seen Shana since she was nine months old.

This lady from New York asked if Rafiah could see Shana if she could fly to New York and then drive to Virginia. We assured the woman that we would love to have Rafiah come and visit Shana, but "do not inform Ron of your plans," we warned her. For some reason she has not made the trip. I don't know the exact reason, whether she did not have the funds, could not get a visa, or did not want to leave her other children.

For a few months after her graduation from Paris Island, Shana was stationed at Cherry Point, North Carolina. During this time she was sent to the Pensacola Naval Air Station for some additional training. While there she celebrated her nineteenth birthday by going skydiving with an instructor. (Brave kid, eh?) Then she was transferred to Yuma, Arizona, where she spent a little over a year before being sent to Kuwait for about six months where she helped load rockets and bombs on Harrier jump jets and F-16's during the invasion of Iraq.

By the time her tour of duty was up, she had decided to marry one of her Marine comrades in Las Vegas, Nevada. Sheryl and I flew out and participated in the wedding. Sheryl had prepared most of the decorations and shipped them on ahead, and I had the privilege of giving her away although she preferred to walk the isle by herself.

When Shana's husband was discharged they settled in Washington State to be near his parents. We visited them in 2005. They now have two beautiful children, a boy born in May 2006 and a girl born in May 2008. Shana was expecting her firstborn, under doctors orders not to travel, and was unable to be with our family when Sheryl was on her deathbed. However, a call was placed to her so she could say her good-byes just a couple of days before Sheryl's passing in April 2006.

She brought my new grandson to visit me in October 2007 and I now have pictures of my new granddaughter as well. They are both beautiful children, just as she was and I am thankful that they have a stable home with two loving parents. I am proud of the woman Shana has become and am thankful to have been given the opportunity to play such a major role in her life.

We thought Ron had finally learned his lesson and would finally leave us alone, but guess what? The sleeping dog woke up again. On January 25, 2009, Ron filed another twenty million dollar lawsuit against a sheriff's investigator, my son Jake, me, and about thirty other defendants, that he claimed were allied with us in the kidnapping of his daughter Shana and the subsequent cover up, which of course never happened, but he'll never be convinced; his head is like a rock.

Jake informed me that my Social Security number was on Ron's websites (five or six of them!) along with my wife's and her sister's (both now deceased). Ron had also published our full names and dates of birth setting us up for identity theft, which I suspect was his malicious intent. I notified an officer who investigated computer crimes. He looked into it and found some accusations against federal officials as well. Those could be classified as felonies. He contacted Ron's servers/web providers and informed them that these accusations had to be removed from the websites within forty-eight hours or the websites would be shut down. Failure to comply would make them subject to arrest. Apparently, Ron balked or refused and as a result all or most of his websites were shut down including his e-mail address.

Included in the list of defendants in the lawsuit besides my son Jake, the investigator, and me, were the current and former sheriff, both of our former Presidents, George Bush and George W. Bush, employees of the Justice Department and the State Department, F. B. I. agents, and about every judge and lawyer in the Amherst County and Lynchburg areas who ever ruled against him or disagreed with him. There were numerous others as well.

Needless to say, when the judge assigned to the case studied it, and several other lawsuits Ron had filed about almost identical claims, the judge did what some of the other judges had done; he dismissed it without a hearing. He labeled it as "obviously frivolous," "unsubstantial," "absolutely devoid of merit," and "no longer open to discussion."

Even now, it is not a time to stop praying. We encouraged Shana to pray for her father. We still pray for God's guidance and protection. We pray for Ron's salvation and for Shana and her family to grow in the Lord. Even though I know the Lord was in control, as He always is, everything is still hard for me to believe. However, God always knew what the outcome would be.

Scripture References

1). Genesis 3:4-5 "And the serpent said unto the woman, 'Ye shall not surely die; For God doth know that in the day ye eat thereof, then your eyes shall be opened, and ye shall be as gods, knowing good and evil.'"

2). Genesis 16:12 "And he will be a wild man; his hand will be against every man, and every man's hand against him."

3). Genesis 16:15 "And Hagar bare Abram a son: and Abram called his son's name, which Hagar bare, Ishmael."

4). Genesis 21:9 - 10 "And Sara saw the son of Hagar the Egyptian which she had born unto Abraham, mocking. Wherefore she said unto Abraham, 'Cast out this bondwoman and her son; for the son of the bondwoman shall not be heir with my son, even with Isaac.'"

5). Exodus 32:11-14 "And Moses besought the Lord his God and said, Lord, why doth thy wrath wax hot against thy people, which thou has brought forth out of the land of Egypt with great power, and with a mighty hand? Wherefore should the Egyptians speak, and say, 'For mischief did he bring them out, to slay them in the mountains, and to consume them from the face of the earth? Turn from thy fierce wrath, and repent of this evil against thy people. Remember Abraham, Isaac, and Israel, thy servants, to whom thou swarest by thine own self, and saidest unto them, "I will multiply your seed as the stars of heaven, and all this land that I have spoken of will I give unto your seed, and they shall inherit it forever."' And the Lord repented of the evil which he thought to do unto his people."

6). Exodus 32:32 "Yet now, if thou wilt forgive their sin; and if not, blot me, I pray thee, out of thy book which thou hast written."

7). Deuteronomy 6:6-7 "And these words, which I command thee this day, shall be in thine heart: and thou shalt teach them diligently unto thy children and shalt talk of them when thou sittest in thine house, and when thou walkest by the way, and when thou liest down, and when thou risest up."

8). Deuteronomy 11:19 "And ye shall teach them your children, speaking of them when thou sittest in thine house, and when thou walkest by the way, and when thou liest down, and when thou risest up."

9). Psalms 7:11b "God is angry with the wicked everyday."

10). Psalms 34:7 "The angel of the Lord encampeth round about them that fear him, and delivereth them."

11). Psalms 139:2-4 "Thou knowest my downsitting and mine uprising, thou understandest my thought afar off. Thou compassest my path and my lying down, and art acquainted with all my ways. For there is not a word in my tongue, but, lo, O Lord, thou knowest it altogether."

12). Proverbs 3:5-6 "Trust in the Lord with all thine heart; and lean not unto thine own understanding. In all thy ways acknowledge Him, and he shall direct thy paths."

13). Proverbs 16:9 "A man's heart deviseth his way; but the Lord directeth his steps."

14). Proverbs 16:33 "The lot is cast into the lap; but the whole disposing thereof is of the Lord."

15). Proverbs 20:24 "Man's goings are of the Lord; how can a man then understand his own way?"

16). Proverbs 21:1 "The king's heart is in the hand of the Lord, as the rivers of water; he turneth it whithersoever he will."

17). Proverbs 22:6 "Train up a child in the way he should go; and when he is old, he will not depart from it."

18). Proverbs 26:12 "Seest thou a man wise in his own conceit? There is more hope of a fool than of him."

19). Proverbs 28:26 "He that trusteth in his own heart is a fool; but whoso walketh wisely, he shall be delivered."

20). Isaiah 55:8-9 "For my thoughts are not your thoughts, neither are your ways my ways, saith the Lord. For as the heavens are higher than the earth, so are my ways higher than your ways and my thoughts than your thoughts."

21). Jeremiah 10:23 "O Lord, I know that the way of man is not in himself; it is not in man that walketh to direct his steps."

22). Jeremiah 17:9 "The heart is deceitful above all things, and desperately wicked; who can know it?"

23). Jeremiah 33:3 "Call unto me, and I will answer thee, and shew thee great and mighty things which thou knowest not."

24). Lamentations 3:37 "Who is he that saith, and it cometh to pass, when the Lord commandeth it not?"

25). Daniel 4:32b "Until thou know that the most High ruleth in the kingdom of men, and giveth it to whomsoever he will."

26). Daniel 4:35 "And he doeth according to his will in the armies of heaven, and among the inhabitants of the earth; and none can stay his hand, or say unto him what doest thou?"

27). Matthew 7:7-8 "Ask, and it shall be given you; seek, and ye shall find: knock, and it shall be opened unto you; for every one that asketh receiveth; and he that seeketh findeth; and to him that knocketh it shall be opened."

28). Matthew 11:25 "I thank thee, o Father, Lord of heaven and earth, because thou has hid these things from the wise and prudent, and has revealed them unto babes."

29). Matthew 12:30 "He that is not with me is against me; and he that gathereth not with me scattereth abroad."

30). Matthew 18:14 "Even so it is not the will of your father which is in heaven, that one of these little ones should perish."

31). Mark 4:19 "And the cares of this world, and the deceitfulness of riches, and the lusts of other things entering in, choke the word, and it becometh unfruitful."

32). Mark 9:42 "And whosoever shall offend one of these little ones that believe in me, it is better for him that a millstone were hanged about his neck, and he were cast into the sea."

33). Mark 10:14-15 "...Suffer the little children to come unto me, and forbid them not: for of such is the kingdom of God. Verily I say unto you, whosoever shall not receive the kingdom of God as a little child, he shall not enter therein."

34). Mark 11:24 "Therefore I say unto you, what things soever ye desire, when you pray, believe that ye receive them, and ye shall have them."

35). John 1:12-13 "But as many as received him, to them gave he power to become the sons of God, even to them that believe on his name; which were born, not of blood, nor of the will of the flesh, nor of the will of man, but of God."

36). John 3:3 "Verily, verily, I say unto thee, Except a man be born again, he cannot see the kingdom of God."

37). John 3:7 "Marvel not that I said unto thee, Ye must be born again."

38). Acts 2:23 "Him being delivered by the determinate counsel and foreknowledge of God, ye have taken, and by wicked hands have crucified and slain."

39). Romans 3:4a "God forbid; yea, let God be true, but every man a liar..."

40). Acts 4:28 "For to do whatsoever thy hand and thy counsel determined before to be done."

41). Romans 8:28 "And we know that all things work together for good to them that love God to them who are the called according to his purpose."

42). Romans 12:3 "For I say through the grace given unto me, to every man that is among you, not to think of himself more highly than he ought to think; but to think soberly, according as God hath dealt to every man the measure of faith."

43). I Corinthians 8:2 "And if any man think that he knoweth anything, he knoweth nothing yet as he ought to know."

44). Galatians 5:8 "This persuasion cometh not of him that calleth you."

45). Ephesians 4:23 "And be renewed in the spirit of your mind."

46). Ephesians 4: 4:30 "And grieve not the Holy Spirit of God, whereby ye are sealed unto the day of redemption."

47). Ephesians 6:4b "But bring them up in the nurture and admonition of the Lord."

48). I Timothy 2:4 "Who will have all men to be saved, and come unto the knowledge of the truth."

49). I Timothy 5:8 "But if any provide not for his own, and specially for those of his own house, he hath denied the faith, and is worse than an infidel."

50). Hebrews 2:3a "How shall we escape, if we neglect so great salvations...?"

51). James 1:8 "A double minded man is unstable in all his ways."

52). 1 Peter 2:2 "As newborn babes, desire the sincere milk of the word, that ye may grow thereby."

53). II Peter 3:9 "The Lord is not slack concerning his promise, as some men count slackness; but is longsuffering to us-ward, not willing that any should perish, but that all should come to repentance."

To order more copies visit
www.roneil.books.officelive.com